Edexcel International GCSE English Language A

Edexcel Certificate in English Language

Revision Guide

Anna O'Kennedy

Published by Pearson Education Limited, Edinburgh Gate, Harlow, Essex, CM20 2JE.

www.pearsonglobalschools.com

Copies of official specifications for all Edexcel qualifications may be found on the Edexcel website: www.edexcel.com

Text © Pearson Education Limited 2013
Edited by Hazel Harris
Proofread by Jane Hammett
Original design by Richard Ponsford
Typeset by Phoenix Photosetting
Original illustrations © Pearson Education Limited 2013
Indexed by Indexing Specialists (UK) Ltd.

The right of Anna O'Kennedy to be identified as author of this work has been asserted by her in accordance with the Copyright, Designs and Patents Act 1988.

First published 2013

17 16 15 14 13
IMP 10 9 8 7 6 5 4 3 2 1

British Library Cataloguing in Publication Data
A catalogue record for this book is available from the British Library

ISBN 978 1 446 90575 3

Printed in Spain by Graficas Estella.

Acknowledgements
We are grateful to the following for permission to reproduce copyright material:

Screenshots
Screenshot on page 10 from http://www.greenpeace.org/international/en/campaigns/climate-change/, © GREENPEACE 2012, Greenpeace; Screenshot on Unprepared non-fiction worksheet 1 from http://www.oxfam.org.uk/get-involved/campaign-with-us/our-campaigns/grow?intcmp=hp_14_wwd4_grow_2012-04-30, reproduced with the permission of Oxfam GB, Oxfam House, John Smith Drive, Cowley, Oxford OX4 2JY, UK www.oxfam.org.uk. Oxfam GB does not necessarily endorse any text or activities that accompany the materials.

Text
Extract on pages 3–5 from *Touching the Void*, Vintage (Random House) (Simpson J), The Random House Group (UK), Touching the Void, Vintage (Random House) (Simpson J); Extract on pages 7–8 from http://rnli.org, RNLI, REPRODUCED BY PERMISSION OF THE RNLI; Article on pages 12–13 from Climate Change: The Facts, *The Guardian* (Ravilious K), http://www.guardian.co.uk/science/2008/apr/28/scienceofclimatechange2, Guardian News and Media Ltd; Extract on pages 19–20 from A Passage to Africa, Little Brown & Agent Hanbury (Alagiah G), Little, Brown Book Group (UK) and THE HANBURY AGENCY LTD; Article on pages 27–28 from Explorers, or Boys Messing About? Either Way, Taxpayer Gets Rescue Bill, *The Guardian* (Morris S), Guardian News and Media Ltd; Extract on pages 30–31 from *Taking on the World*, Penguin (Ellen MacArthur), Penguin Books Ltd and A P Watt at United Agents on behalf of EM (IOW) Ltd; Extract on pages 33–35 from *Chinese Cinderella*, Abridged Ed ed., Puffin; (Yen Mah A),Penguin Books Ltd ; Poetry on pages 38–39 from *Wilfred Owen: The War Poems* Chatto & Windus (Edited by Stallworthy J 1994); Poetry on page 41 from *The Poetry of Robert Frost*, Random House (Edited by Edward Connery Lathem), The Random House Group (UK); Poetry on pages 47–48 adapted from *Electricity Comes to Cocoa Bottom*, Peepal Tree Press Ltd (Douglas M); Extract on page 55, Section B worksheet 5 and Worksheet King Schariar and his Brother from *Arabian Nights*, AFRICAN-AMERICAN CHRONICLE (LANG, ANDREW), Chronicle Books; Extract on page 51 and Section B worksheet 4 from *Veronica* (Maja-Pearce A), Adewale Maja-Pearce; Extract on page 60 adapted from *Dark Star Safari*, Penguin (Theroux, P 2002), The Wylie Agency (UK)

The publisher would like to thank the following for their kind permission to reproduce their photographs in the book and e-book:

(Key: b-bottom; c-centre; l-left; r-right; t-top)

Bridgeman Art Library Ltd: 55tr; **Fotolia.com**: alefilly 53tr, Edyta Pawlowska 58tr, Greg Epperson 5tr, lightpoet 80cl, Sergey Melnikov 59cr, Studiotouch 45tl, TheSupe87 vicl, tomalu 48tl; **Getty Images**: AFP 17tr, 51tr, Archive Photos 41tr, David McLain 24b, Getty Images 21tl, 31c, Getty Images 21tl, 31c, Hulton Archive 39br, 43tr, 49tr, Hulton Archive 39br, 43tr, 49tr, Sue Flood 27tr, Time & Life Pictures 52tl

All other images © Pearson Education

In some instances we have been unable to trace the owners of copyright material, and we would appreciate any information that would enable us to do so. Any omissions will be rectified in subsequent printings if notice is given to the publishers.

Websites
Pearson Education Limited is not responsible for the content of any external internet sites. It is essential for tutors to preview each website before using it in class so as to ensure that the URL is still accurate, relevant and appropriate. We suggest that tutors bookmark useful websites and consider enabling students to access them through the school/college intranet.

A note from the publisher
In order to ensure that this resource offers high-quality support for the associated Edexcel qualification, it has been through a review process by the awarding organisation to confirm that it fully covers the teaching and learning content of the specification or part of a specification at which it is aimed, and demonstrates an appropriate balance between the development of subject skills, knowledge and understanding, in addition to preparation for assessment.

While the publishers have made every attempt to ensure that advice on the qualification and its assessment is accurate, the official specification and associated assessment guidance materials are the only authoritative source of information and should always be referred to for definitive guidance.

Edexcel examiners have not contributed to any sections in this resource relevant to examination papers for which they have responsibility.

No material from an endorsed resource will be used verbatim in any assessment set by Edexcel.

Endorsement of a resource does not mean that the resource is required to achieve this Edexcel qualification, nor does it mean that it is the only suitable material available to support the qualification, and any resource lists produced by the awarding organisation shall include this and other appropriate resources.

Contents

How to Use This Revision Guide

This revision guide has been written for students taking the International GCSE English Language Specification A or Edexcel Certificate in English Language. It is designed to help students to be able to revise the key skills that they will need for exams. Please note that all page references to the student book are correct for student book impression 6 and onwards.

Why is revision important?

Some students feel that it is difficult to revise for English, as there are not straightforward items of information to remember and then recall in the exam. This, however, is false and there are many revision strategies that will help students to succeed in their exams.

How will this book support your revision?

- There is information on the strategies and skills required to succeed in the International GCSE English Language Specification A and the Edexcel Certificate in English Language.

- Worked examples and examiner feedback will help you to structure your own responses.

- Top tips will give you more of an idea about what you will face in your assessments.

- Using the worksheets and interactive quizzes on the e-book that accompanies this revision guide will help you to practise the skills that you will be tested on.

In this book you will work through each part of your assessment for the International GCSE English Language Specification A and the Edexcel Certificate in English Language. You can start wherever you wish – you do not have to study the topics in the order of the book – but remember to study each part.

The glossary explains key words students should understand. All glossary terms have been made bold the first time they appear in the book.

Anthology texts

You will be expected to answer questions on one text from the Section A anthology texts and one text from the Section B anthology texts. Here are some tips on how to revise for these:

- Ensure you have a thorough knowledge of the texts. You should be fully prepared to answer questions on their content, purpose, intended **audience**, stylistic features and structure.

- Be confident that you can answer questions on any text from Section A or Section B – if you prepare only for some, you are cutting down your chances of success as these may not come up in your exam.

- Practise answering questions on the texts so that you know the kinds of questions you will face in exam conditions.

Unprepared non-fiction texts

You will be expected to be able to answer questions on a non-fiction text that you have never seen before. You must practise the skills that you will need for this in order to do it effectively under exam conditions:

- Practise reading for meaning – in this guide you will be given tips on how to do this and what kinds of skills you need to work on.

- Be confident that you know what you are looking for in an unseen text.

- Practise answering questions on unseen non-fiction so that you become confident about how to do this well.

Writing in a wide range of forms and genres

In both coursework (International GCSE English Language Specification A) and in the exams (both specifications) you will have to demonstrate that you can write well for different audiences and in different genres. In order to revise for this you will need to:

- study existing texts to consider what the required style is for different genres and audiences

- practise writing in different styles and genres, aimed at various audiences and employing different techniques.

Top tips for revision

Here are some tips to make your revision successful:

- Prepare your work environment. It is best to work in a place where you can have peace and calm, and not be surrounded by mess or distraction. Put your mobile phone on silent or leave it elsewhere to minimise distractions.

- Work in a quiet environment. Doing this will allow you to remember more of what you revise, so switch off the TV, the radio and your MP3 player.

- Be methodical. Make a plan for your revision and stick to it.

- Revise in short chunks. If you work in concentrated bursts of about an hour, allowing yourself breaks in between, you will remember more than if you sit down for three hours at a time.

- Use visual aids. Colour, pictures and diagrams can help your memory. You could put these up around your room to help the ideas stick in your brain.

- Write, write, write! Practising a skill over and over again can help you to improve how you do it and can help you to remember key points. Don't copy out chunks of text – try to use exam questions under timed conditions, or copy out your annotations on a text. This will help you to remember key points as well as to hone your skills.

- Seek help. You are not alone. It is worth asking parents or teachers for input – if you work through a practice paper, ask someone to mark it for you and get some feedback.

Top tips for the exam

Once you have completed your revision and are in the exam hall, there are still some things that you can do to help yourself:

- Think about your timings in the exam. Ensure you can see a clock or a watch and think about how long you have for each section of the paper.

- Read every question through carefully before you start to answer. It is surprising how many students lose marks by answering a question they think they have seen rather than the one that is printed on the paper.

- Use active reading skills. This ensures you are taking all the information out of a text. To find out what active reading skills are, have a look at the chapter on unprepared non-fiction.

- Plan your answers. Planning answers to the higher-mark questions will ensure that you cover all the important aspects and that your work is organised.

- Be technical. Know your technical terms and use them. Use the glossaries in this book and in the student book to help you to revise these terms.

- Keep it neat. If the examiner can't read your work, it will be difficult to mark it.

- Think about accuracy in spelling, punctuation and structure.

- Don't walk out without reading over your answers! Leave time at the end to read through what you have written. Many students lose marks by forgetting key points that they could have spotted if they had read their work through.

The assessment and what to expect

The following table gives you an outline of the areas of assessment and where in this revision guide you can find more information on them:

Specification	Assessment details	Where to find guidance
International GCSE Specification A (4EAO)	**PAPER 1** (2 hours 15 minutes)	
	Section A: Unprepared passage (Reading)	Chapter 3: Unprepared Non-fiction Pages 57–64
	Section B: One piece from Section A of anthology (Reading)	Chapter 1: Section A Anthology Texts Pages 1–36
	Writing task based on topic of chosen passage from Section A of anthology	
	Section C: Inform, explain, describe (Writing)	Chapter 4: Writing to inform, explain, describe Pages 73–74
	PAPER 2 (1 hour 30 minutes)	
	Question 1: One piece from Section B of anthology (Reading)	Chapter 2: Section B Anthology Texts Pages 37–56
	Question 2: (Writing)	Chapter 4: Writing in a Wide Range of Forms and Genres Pages 65–78
	Either:	
	Explore, imagine, entertain	Chapter 4: Writing to explore, imagine, entertain Pages 70–73
	Or:	
	Argue, persuade, advise	Chapter 4: Writing to argue, persuade, advise Pages 74–77

Specification	Assessment details	Where to find guidance
Certificate Level 1/Level 2 (KEAO)	**PAPER 1** (2 hours 15 minutes)	
	Section A: Unprepared passage (Reading)	Chapter 3: Unprepared Non-fiction Pages 57–64
	Section B: One piece from Section A of anthology (Reading) Writing task based on topic of chosen passage from Section A of anthology	Chapter 1: Section A Anthology Texts Pages 1–36
	Section C: Inform, explain, describe (Writing)	Chapter 4: Writing to inform, explain, describe Pages 73–74
	PAPER 2 (1 hour 30 minutes)	
	Question 1: One piece from Section B of anthology (Reading)	Chapter 2: Section B Anthology Texts Pages 37–56
	Question 2: (Writing) Two tasks (Question 2a and Question 2b)	Chapter 4: Writing in a Wide Range of Forms and Genres Pages 65–78
	• Explore, imagine, entertain	Chapter 4: Writing to explore, imagine, entertain Pages 70–73
	• Argue, persuade, advise	Chapter 4: Writing to argue, persuade, advise Pages 74–77

Chapter 1: Section A Anthology Texts

Introduction

In this section of the revision guide we will look at each of the Section A anthology texts for International GCSE English Language Specification A and the Edexcel Certificate in English Language. For each extract we will look at the way in which the piece has been written, and focus on the three vital elements:

- Purpose: Why has the piece been written and what is it trying to communicate?

- Audience: Who is the piece intended for and how can we identify this?

- Technique: What are the different features that the writer uses in the text to make it engaging for the reader?

There are accompanying worksheets for this section of the revision guide that will guide you through some exam-style questions for these texts and help you to do some exploration of your own.

Know your assessment objective

In this part of the exam you will be demonstrating that you can achieve the objectives set out below. On the left are the assessment objectives and on the right there are interpretations of each aspect.

AO2 (i): Read and understand texts with insight and engagement.	Demonstrate that you *understand* the text, and can use *quotations* and references to show that you have formed your own *interesting ideas* about it.
AO2 (ii): Develop and sustain interpretations of writers' ideas and perspectives.	Show that you understand what the writer is trying to communicate and show that you know what is *reality* and what are the writer's *feelings*.
AO2 (iii): Understand and make some evaluation of how writers use linguistic and structural devices to achieve their effects.	Discuss how *effective writers' choices* are on a *word, sentence and text level* in creating a desired *effect*.

What the examiner wants

You need to be able to communicate to the examiner that you can fulfil the brief of the assessment objectives. There are several ways that you can ensure you do this. The examiner wants to see:

- clear, concise answers that fully address the question

- answers that meet the needs of the question – a three-mark question does not demand a whole essay as an answer (the number of lines in the answer booklet of your exam paper should be a good guide)

- a clear understanding of the text

- a specific focus on language and structural techniques that create an effect

- quotations from the text that have clear references and are appropriate for the answer you give.

How to use quotations

Assessment objective 2 (ii) demands that you use 'appropriate reference to texts', which means that you must use quotations or close references to back up what you say. Here are some tips on using quotations – a skill you will need throughout this section of the revision guide:

- Use only those quotations that actually support your ideas. Don't just quote for the sake of it; find a piece that backs up your own interpretations of the text and comment on the effects of key words.

- A quotation can come from direct speech, indirect speech or any other part of the writing.

- Don't copy out a huge chunk of the text; sometimes the best quotation can be just a few words.

- Always use speech marks to surround your quotation to demonstrate that it is taken from the text.

Active reading

As you read through the extracts, you should be highlighting any interesting features that the writer has used to have an impact on the reader. These could be:

- vocabulary choices that affect the reader

- technical features that might be used to influence the way you read the text

- interesting punctuation choices that could be explained as having an impact on the audience

- **sentence** structures that have been used to create an effect of some kind

- the way in which the text has been structured – any use of flashback or unusual **chronological** features, or non-standard paragraphing.

Notes

Touching the Void (pages 1–5 in the student book)

- *Touching the Void* is a book by Joe Simpson.

- It was published in 1988.

- It was made into an award-winning documentary film in 2003.

- It tells the story of Joe and his climbing partner Simon Yates attempting to climb Siula Grande in Peru.

- Joe breaks his leg and finds himself dangling from the end of a rope over a precipice. Simon is forced to cut the rope to save himself and climbs down the mountain, believing Joe is dead.

- Against all odds, Joe crawls down the mountain and is finally rescued.

- This extract gives an account from both climbers of the accident.

Joe's account

I hit the slope at the base of the cliff before I saw it coming. I was facing into the slope and both knees locked as I struck it. I felt a shattering blow in my knee, felt bones splitting, and screamed. The impact catapulted me over backwards and down the slope of the East Face. I slid, head-first, on my back. The rushing speed of it confused me. I thought of the drop below but felt nothing. Simon would be ripped off the mountain. He couldn't hold this. I screamed again as I jerked to a sudden violent stop.

Everything was still, silent. My thoughts raced madly. Then pain flooded down my thigh – a fierce burning fire coming down the inside of my thigh, seeming
10 to ball in my groin, building and building until I cried out at it, and my breathing came in ragged gasps. My leg!... My leg!

I hung, head down, on my back, left leg tangled in the rope above me and my right leg hanging slackly to one side. I lifted my head from the snow and stared, up across my chest, at a grotesque distortion in the right knee, twisting the leg into a strange zigzag. I didn't connect it with the pain which burnt my groin. That had nothing to do with my knee. I kicked my left leg free of the rope and swung round until I was hanging against the snow on my chest, feet down. The pain eased. I kicked my left foot into the slope and stood up.

20 A wave of nausea surged over me. I pressed my face into the snow, and the sharp cold seemed to calm me. Something terrible, something dark with dread occurred to me, and as I thought about it I felt the dark thought break into panic: 'I've broken my leg, that's it. I'm dead. Everyone said it... if there's just two of you a broken ankle could turn into a death sentence... if it's broken... if... It doesn't hurt so much, maybe I've just ripped something.'

I kicked my right leg against the slope, feeling sure it wasn't broken. My knee exploded. Bone grated, and the fireball rushed from groin to knee. I screamed. I looked down at the knee and could see it was broken, yet I tried not to believe what I was seeing. It wasn't just broken, it was ruptured, twisted, crushed,
30 and I could see the kink in the joint and knew what had happened. The impact had driven my lower leg up through the knee joint. ...

I dug my axes into the snow, and pounded my good leg deeply into the soft slope until I felt sure it wouldn't slip. The effort brought back the nausea and I felt my head spin giddily to the point of fainting. I moved and a searing spasm of pain cleared away the faintness. I could see the summit of Seria Norte away to the west. I was not far below it. The sight drove home how desperately things had changed. We were above 19,000 feet, still on the ridge, and very much alone. I looked south at the small rise I had hoped to scale quickly and it seemed to grow with every second that I stared. I would never get over it.

40 Simon would not be able to get me up it. He would leave me. He had no choice. I held my breath, thinking about it. Left here? Alone?... For an age I felt overwhelmed at the notion of being left; I felt like screaming, and I felt like swearing, but stayed silent. If I said a word, I would panic. I could feel myself teetering on the edge of it.

Simon's account

Joe had disappeared behind a rise in the ridge and began moving faster than I could go. I was glad we had put the steep section behind us at last. ... I felt tired and was grateful to be able to follow Joe's tracks instead of breaking trail*.

breaking trail: being in front

I rested a while when I saw that Joe had stopped moving. Obviously he had found an obstacle and I thought I would wait until he started moving again.

50 When the rope moved again I trudged forward after it, slowly.

Suddenly there was a sharp tug as the rope lashed out taut across the slope. I was pulled forward several feet as I pushed my axes into the snow and braced myself for another jerk. Nothing happened. I knew that Joe had fallen, but I couldn't see him, so I stayed put. I waited for about ten minutes until the tautened rope went slack on the snow and I felt sure that Joe had got his weight off me. I began to move along his footsteps cautiously, half expecting something else to happen. I kept tensed up and ready to dig my axes in at the first sign of trouble.

As I crested the rise, I could see down a slope to where the rope disappeared
60 over the edge of a drop. I approached slowly, wondering what had happened. When I reached the top of the drop I saw Joe below me. He had one foot dug in and was leaning against the slope with his face buried in the snow. I asked him what had happened and he looked at me in surprise. I knew he was injured, but the significance didn't hit me at first.

He told me very calmly that he had broken his leg. He looked pathetic, and my immediate thought came without any emotion. ... You're dead... no two ways about it! I think he knew it too. I could see it in his face. It was all totally rational. I knew where we were, I took in everything around me instantly, and knew he was dead. It never occurred to me that I might also die. I
70 accepted without question that I could get off the mountain alone. I had no doubt about that.

... Below him I could see thousands of feet of open face falling into the eastern glacier bay. I watched him quite dispassionately. I couldn't help him, and it occurred to me that in all likelihood he would fall to his death. I wasn't disturbed by the thought. In a way I hoped he would fall. I knew I couldn't leave him while he was still fighting for it, but I had no idea how I might help him. I could get down. If I tried to get him down I might die with him. It didn't frighten me. It just seemed a waste. It would be pointless. I kept staring at him, expecting him to fall...

Joe Simpson

Points you may want to consider about this extract

- Both men have different motivations for telling their stories – we can only guess at what these are.

- Anything that is written after the fact is subject to hindsight.

- The book was written to sell; it is not a newspaper article but a book that tells an exciting adventure story. This may change the way in which the **facts** are presented.

Have a look at the tables below. The first suggests the intended purpose of the text, the second considers audience and the third discusses the techniques the author uses. You should copy and complete these tables and try to add to them yourself.

Purpose

Why has the text been written?	Evidence	Effect on the reader
To give the reader a flavour of what it would be like to be in a situation like this.	Both accounts are written in the first person using the pronoun 'I'.	
To retell the story of what happened.		

Audience

Who is the text aimed at?	Evidence	Effect on the reader
People who are interested in mountaineering.		
Anyone who likes a thrilling story.		

Techniques

What kinds of devices are used to create effect?	Evidence	Effect on the reader
Vocabulary is chosen for effect.		
Sibilance.		
Metaphor.		
Simple sentences.		

Some questions to help you revise the extract

1. See if you can find the following in the text and then explain how they have an effect on the reader:

- **metaphor**
- use of sentence structure to create a specific effect
- punctuation used to create tension.

2. How effective is it to have both Simon's and Joe's **viewpoints** here?

3. How do you relate to the two different climbers? Why?

4. Other than the points mentioned in the grid above, what is the purpose of this extract?

Notes

Your Guide To Beach Safety (pages 5–9 in the student book)

- The RNLI is the Royal National Lifeboat Institution.
- It is a charitable organisation that saves lives at sea in the UK and Republic of Ireland.
- Not only does it supply coastguards and lifeboats but it also raises awareness of potential dangers of the sea.
- It produces leaflets, information videos and other materials to help members of the public to stay safe when they use beaches.

THE RNLI

The Royal National Lifeboat Institution is the charity that saves lives at sea.

LIFEBOATS AND LIFEGUARDS

We operate over 230 lifeboat stations in the UK and RoI and have over 330 lifeboats in service, 24 hours a day, 365 days a year. Since the RNLI was founded in 1824, our volunteer lifeboat crews have saved more than 137,000 lives – rescuing around 8,000 people every year.

Our seasonal lifeguard service now operates on more than 100 beaches in the UK. It responds to more than 9,000 incidents a year and is planned to double its coverage by 2010.

FUNDED BY YOU

As a charity, the RNLI relies on voluntary financial support including legacies, which help fund 6 out of 10 launches. With more people using our beaches and seas, the demand on our services is greater than ever and our running costs average over £335,000 a day.

LIFESAVING ADVICE AND INFORMATION

A range of free resources and practical advice is available to promote sea, beach and commercial fishing safety and to support primary and secondary school teachers. For further information call **0800 543210** or visit **rnli.org.uk.**

ORDINARY PEOPLE, EXTRAORDINARY ACTS

People from all walks of life help the RNLI to save lives at sea. Thousands of volunteer crew members, shorehelpers, committee members and fundraisers give their time, skill and commitment. They are strongly supported by specialist staff.

Training is vital – it turns volunteers into lifesavers. Every year the RNLI delivers the highest quality of training at The Lifeboat College in Poole and at its lifeboat stations.

BEACHES NEED LIFEGUARDS

Our lifeguards work with lifeboat crews to provide a seamless rescue service from the beach to the open sea.

When someone is drowning inthe surf seconds count, so we need expert lifesavers on the beach ready to act.

As much as 95% of our lifeguards' work is preventative – that is, they look out for potential problems before they develop into something worse, and give proactive advice and information to beachgoers.

The RNLI aims to continue expanding its lifeguard service across the whole country – but we can't achieve this without support from the public.

Every year it costs at least £450 to equip and £900 to train each lifeguard – will you help us meet that need?

Phone 0800 543210 or go to rnli.org.uk to donate now and help save lives at sea. Thank you.

Whether we're rescuing an offshore fisherman or a child swept out to sea, the RNLI exists to save **Life first.**

RNLI LIFEBOATS, LIFEGUARDS LIFE FIRST

Reproduced from the leaflet 'On the Beach' 2008 by permission of the RNLI.

Points you may want to consider about this extract

- A leaflet is not necessarily restricted to one **genre** of writing. It may try to **persuade** you to do something, advise you of something or supply **information**.

- It is important to be able to comment on the language and the layout of a piece like this – also remember that, when writers use different genres, they may also use different styles.

- Think about the order in which the information is presented. Important choices have been made by the writers about where they place the different sections of the text.

Have a look at the tables below. The first suggests the intended purpose of the text, the second considers audience and the third discusses the techniques the author uses. You should copy and complete these tables and try to add to them yourself.

Purpose

Why has the text been written?	Evidence	Effect on the reader
To inform the public about how to enjoy the beach.		

Audience

Who is the text aimed at?	Evidence	Effect on the reader
Anyone who intends to use the beach.		
Families who want to use the beach.		
Watersports enthusiasts.		

Techniques

What kinds of devices are used to create effect?	Evidence	Effect on the reader
Repetition.	'call 999 or 112'.	
Primary colours.	The leaflet uses only primary colours.	
Images.		
	'Always... Never...'	

Some questions to help you revise the extract

1. As well as to inform the public about how to use the beach, what might be another reason that the text was written?

2. How effective do you think it is in communicating its message? Why?

3. See if you can find at least one example of the following in the extract and then explain its effect on the reader:

   - **emotive language**

   - command language

   - statistics.

4. What is the point of using the personal story?

Climate Change web page – Greenpeace UK (pages 9–11 in the student book)

- This web page was produced by Greenpeace, an international campaigning organisation.

- It campaigns on topics such as deforestation, global warming, overfishing and anti-nuclear issues.

- It does not accept government funding but instead relies on its three million supporters and grants.

Source: http://www.greenpeace.org.uk/climate

Points you may want to consider about this extract

- Web pages usually contain more than one kind of writing – in this piece we can see writing to argue, describe, persuade and more.

- Greenpeace has a set agenda and has to raise awareness about it.

- Greenpeace is a huge organisation with good funding.

Have a look at the tables below. The first suggests the intended purpose of the text, the second considers audience and the third discusses the techniques the author uses. You should copy and complete these tables and try to add to them yourself.

Purpose

Why has the text been written?	Evidence	Effect on the reader
To inform the reader.		
To persuade the reader to become involved.		

Audience

Who is the text aimed at?	Evidence	Effect on the reader
Quite well-informed readers.		

Techniques

What kinds of devices are used to create effect?	Evidence	Effect on the reader
Repetition.		
Emotive language.		This kind of vocabulary immediately makes the problem seem like something we should get involved with.
Single-sentence paragraph.		

Some questions to help you revise the extract

1. The text on this website is aimed at a UK audience. Give examples to support this statement.

2. What is the impact of the chosen colour scheme?

3. Why has the author used the phrase 'Take Action'?

4. Select two repeated phrases from the page and explain why they have been repeated.

Climate Change: The Facts (pages 12–15 in the student book)

- This article was published by *The Guardian* newspaper.
- It formed part of a booklet entitled 'Science Course Part III: The Earth'.
- It focuses on global warming.
- Climate change has been a 'hot topic' in the news for several years.

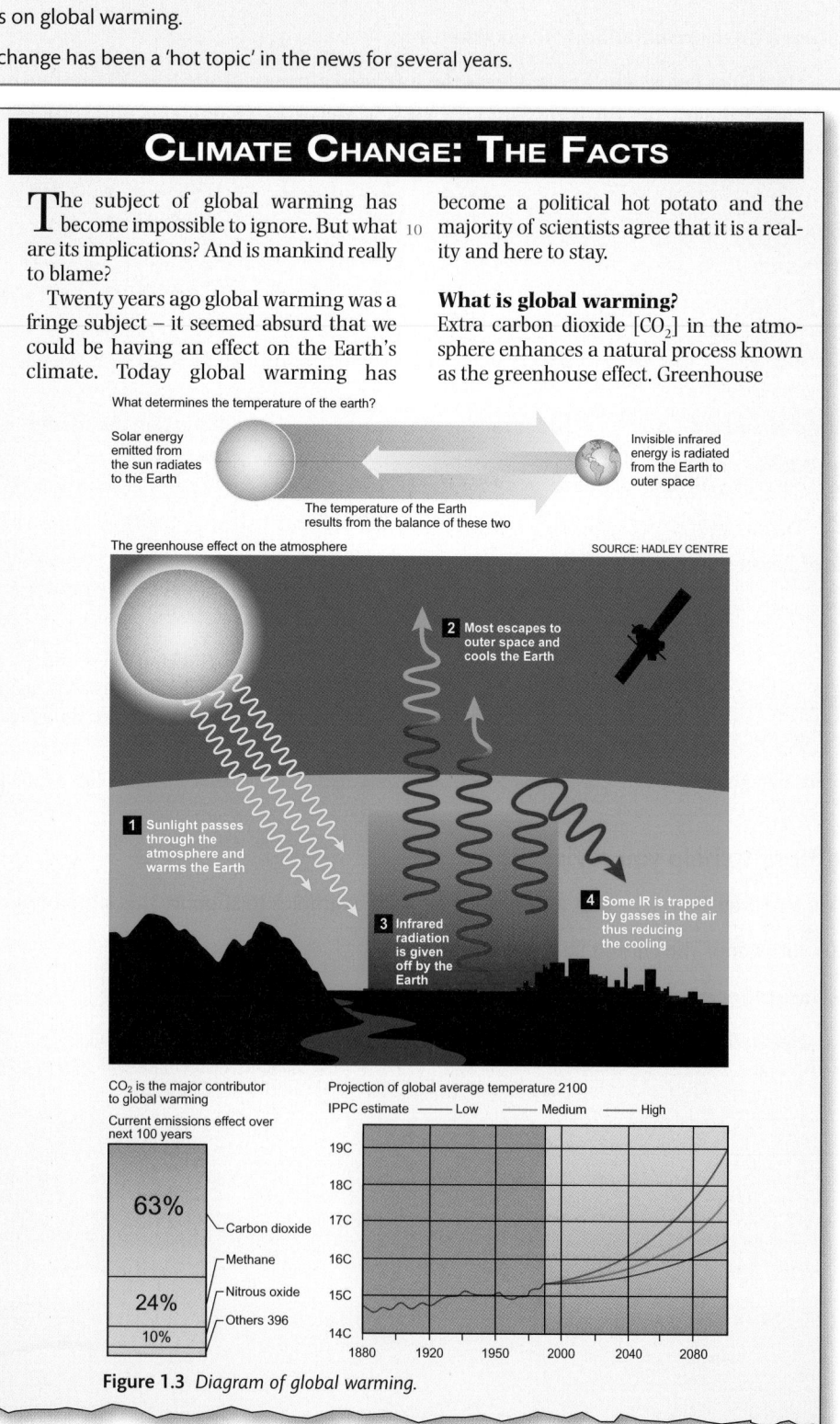

CLIMATE CHANGE: THE FACTS

The subject of global warming has become impossible to ignore. But what are its implications? And is mankind really to blame?

Twenty years ago global warming was a fringe subject – it seemed absurd that we could be having an effect on the Earth's climate. Today global warming has become a political hot potato and the majority of scientists agree that it is a reality and here to stay.

What is global warming?
Extra carbon dioxide [CO_2] in the atmosphere enhances a natural process known as the greenhouse effect. Greenhouse

What determines the temperature of the earth?

Solar energy emitted from the sun radiates to the Earth

Invisible infrared energy is radiated from the Earth to outer space

The temperature of the Earth results from the balance of these two

The greenhouse effect on the atmosphere

SOURCE: HADLEY CENTRE

1 Sunlight passes through the atmosphere and warms the Earth

2 Most escapes to outer space and cools the Earth

3 Infrared radiation is given off by the Earth

4 Some IR is trapped by gasses in the air thus reducing the cooling

CO_2 is the major contributor to global warming

Current emissions effect over next 100 years

63% — Carbon dioxide
— Methane
24% — Nitrous oxide
— Others 396
10%

Projection of global average temperature 2100
IPPC estimate —— Low —— Medium —— High

19C
18C
17C
16C
15C
14C
1880   1920   1950   2000   2040   2080

Figure 1.3 *Diagram of global warming.*

gases, such as carbon dioxide, absorb heat and release it slowly. Without this process, Earth would be too cold for life to survive.

Over the past 200 years mankind has increased the proportion of greenhouse gases in the Earth's atmosphere, primarily by burning fossil fuels. The higher levels of greenhouse gases are causing our planet to warm – global warming.

Is global warming really caused by humans?

Since 1958 scientists at the Mauna Loa Observatory in Hawaii have taken continuous measurements of atmospheric carbon dioxide. The levels go up and down with the seasons, but overall they demonstrate a relentless rise.

Bubbles of gas from ice cores and the chemical composition of fossil shells provide us with a record of atmospheric carbon dioxide going back millions of years. There have been warm periods in the past where carbon dioxide was at levels similar to those seen today. However, the rate of change that we see today is exceptional: carbon dioxide levels have never risen so fast. By 2000 they were 17% higher than in 1959.

Accompanying this rapid increase in carbon dioxide we see a rise in average global temperatures. Warming in the past 100 years has caused about a 0.8°C increase in global average temperature. Eleven of the 12 years in the period 1995–2006 rank among the top 12 warmest years since 1850.

There is little doubt that humanity is responsible for the rapid rise in carbon dioxide levels. The rise in temperatures that has accompanied our fossil fuel addiction seems too much of a coincidence to be just chance. Most people now agree that our actions are having an effect on Earth's climate.

How hot will it get?

Estimates from some of the world's best climate scientists – the Inter-governmental Panel on Climate Change (IPCC) – suggest that the average global temperature will have risen between 2.5°C and 10.4°C by 2100.

Whether it will be the lower or upper end of this estimate is unclear. Currently, oceans and trees are helping to mop up some of the heat by absorbing carbon dioxide, but eventually they will reach capacity and be unable to absorb more. At this point the atmosphere will take the full load, potentially pushing temperatures sky high.

Is it just carbon dioxide we need to worry about?

No. Carbon dioxide is just one of a number of greenhouse gases, which include water vapour, methane, nitrous oxide and ozone. Livestock farming (farting cows) and rice paddy farming (rotting vegetation) have contributed to higher levels of methane in the atmosphere.

What is more, methane has a nasty sting in its tail. Although it only hangs around in the atmosphere for about 10 years, it is far more potent as a greenhouse gas, trapping about 20 times as much heat as carbon dioxide.

What are tipping points?

A steady rise in greenhouse gases won't necessarily cause a steady rise in global temperatures. Earth's climate is highly complicated and scientists fear that many delicate thresholds exist, which once passed could trigger a dramatic change. These thresholds have become known as 'tipping points'.

One potential trigger could be the release of methane from methane clathrate compounds buried on the sea floor. Currently these deposits are frozen, but if the oceans warm sufficiently they could melt, burping vast quantities of methane into the atmosphere. Scientists fear that this sudden release may cause a runaway greenhouse effect.

How will global warming affect us?

Although average global temperatures are predicted to rise, this doesn't necessarily mean that we'll be sitting in our deckchairs all year round. The extra energy from the added warmth in the Earth's atmosphere will need to find a release, and the result is likely to be more extreme weather.

If we stop emitting CO_2 now will it get better straight away?

Unfortunately not. Research shows that we are already committed to an average global temperature rise of nearly 1°C, lasting for at least the next 500 years.

Kate Ravilious

Adapted from an article published in the *Guardian* newspaper supplement – 'Science Course Part III: The Earth' (in association with the Science Museum)

One point you may want to consider about this extract

- It was printed in a newspaper and all newspapers have their own point of view.

Have a look at the tables below. The first suggests the intended purpose of the text, the second considers audience and the third discusses the techniques the author uses. You should copy and complete these tables and try to add to them yourself.

Purpose

Why has the text been written?	Evidence	Effect on the reader
To inform the reader about climate change.		

Audience

Who is the text aimed at?	Evidence	Effect on the reader
		The title of the booklet that the piece comes from suggests it is targeting people who have an interest in science.
People who want to learn more about climate change.		
		The use of facts and figures makes it harder to question the writer's authority.

Techniques

What kinds of devices are used to create effect?	Evidence	Effect on the reader
	'But what are the implications? And is mankind really to blame?'	
Emboldened sub-headings.		
Impersonal vocabulary.		

Some questions to help you revise the extract

1. See if you can find at least one example of the following in the extract and then explain its effect on the reader:

   - metaphor

   - punctuation used for effect

   - sentence structures used to build tension in the writing.

2. Why do you think the diagram has been included?

3. What does the title of the booklet ('Science Course Part III') suggest about the intended audience?

A Game of Polo with a Headless Goat (pages 16–20 in the student book)

- Emma Levine is a travel writer who wrote this book as a spin-off from her TV series about strange and unusual sports in Asia.
- The series and book reveal insights not only into the sports but also into the cultures that they belong to.
- This type of writing is called a travelogue.

A Game of Polo with a Headless Goat

We drove off to find the best viewing spot, which turned out to be the crest of the hill so we could see the approaching race. I asked the lads if we could join in the 'Wacky Races' and follow the donkeys, and they loved the idea. 'We'll open the car boot, you climb inside and point your camera towards the race. As the donkeys overtake us, we'll join the cars.' 'But will you try and get to the front?' 'Oh yes, that's no problem.'

The two lads who had never been interested in this Karachi sport were suddenly fired up with enthusiasm. We waited for eternity on the brow of the hill, me perched in the boot with a zoom lens pointing out. Nearly one
10 hour later I was beginning to feel rather silly when the only action was a villager on a wobbly bicycle, who nearly fell off as he cycled past and gazed around at us.

Several vehicles went past, and some donkey-carts carrying spectators. 'Are they coming?' we called out to them. 'Coming, coming,' came the reply. I was beginning to lose faith in its happening, but the lads remained confident.

Just as I was assuming that the race had been cancelled, we spotted two approaching donkey-carts in front of a cloud of fumes and dust created by some fifty vehicles roaring up in their wake. As they drew nearer, Yaqoob revved up
20 the engine and began to inch the car out of the lay-by. The two donkeys were almost dwarfed by their entourage; but there was no denying their speed – the Kibla donkey is said to achieve speeds of up to 40 kph, and this looked close. The two were neck-and-neck, their jockeys perched on top of the tiny carts using their whips energetically, although not cruelly.

The noise of the approaching vehicles grew; horns tooting, bells ringing, and the special rattles used just for this purpose (like maracas, a metal container filled with dried beans). Men standing on top of their cars and vans, hanging out of taxis and perched on lorries, all cheered and shouted, while the vehicles jostled to get to the front of the convoy.

30 Yaqoob chose exactly the right moment to edge out of the road and swerve in front of the nearest car, finding the perfect place to see the two donkeys and at the front of the vehicles. This was Formula One without rules, or a city-centre rush hour gone anarchic*; a complete flouting* of every type of traffic rule and common sense.

*anarchic: lawless
*flouting: breaking

Our young driver relished this unusual test of driving skills. It was survival of the fittest, and depended upon the ability to cut in front of a vehicle with a sharp flick of the steering wheel (no lane discipline here); quick reflexes to spot a gap in the traffic for a couple of seconds; nerves of steel, and an effective horn. There were two races – the motorized spectators at the back; in front, the two donkeys,

40 still running close and amazingly not put off by the uproar just behind them. Ahead of the donkeys, oncoming traffic – for it was a main road – had to dive into the ditch and wait there until we had passed. Yaqoob loved it. We stayed near to the front, his hand permanently on the horn and his language growing more colourful with every vehicle that tried to cut in front.

The road straightened and levelled, and everyone picked up speed as we neared the end of the race. But just as they were reaching the finishing line, the hospital gate, there was a near pile-up as the leading donkey swerved, lost his footing and he and the cart tumbled over. The race was over.

And then the trouble began. I assumed the winner was the one who completed

50 the race but it was not seen that way by everyone. Apart from the two jockeys and 'officials' (who, it turned out, were actually monitoring the race) there were over a hundred punters who had all staked money on the race, and therefore had strong opinions. Some were claiming that the donkey had fallen because the other one had been ridden too close to him. Voices were raised, fists were out and tempers rising. Everyone gathered around one jockey and official, while the bookmakers were trying to insist that the race should be re-run.

Yaqoob and Iqbal were nervous of hanging around a volatile situation. They agreed to find out for me what was happening, ordering me to stay inside the car as they were swallowed up by the crowd. They emerged some time later. 'It's

60 still not resolved,' said Iqbal, 'but it's starting to get nasty. I think we should leave.' As we drove away, Yaqoob reflected on his driving skills. 'I really enjoyed that,' he said as we drove off at a more sedate pace. 'But I don't even have my licence yet because I'm underage!'

They both found this hilarious, but I was glad he hadn't told me before; an inexperienced, underage driver causing a massive pile-up in the middle of the high-stakes donkey race could have caused problems.

Emma Levine

Points you may want to consider about this extract

- It was written to accompany a TV series so this may have an impact on the content of the book. It may rely on people having seen the TV series to understand the context or it may aim to encourage people to watch the TV series.

- A travelogue is an interesting mix of writing to describe, entertain, amuse, inform and perhaps even persuade.

Have a look at the tables below. The first suggests the intended purpose of the text, the second considers audience and the third discusses the techniques the author uses. You should copy and complete these tables and try to add to them yourself.

Donkey racing in Karachi.

Purpose

Why has the text been written?	Evidence	Effect on the reader
To inform the reader.		

Audience

Who is the text aimed at?	Evidence	Effect on the reader
Anyone who is interested in travel and other cultures.		
Sports enthusiasts.		
Anyone who enjoys an amusing story.		

Techniques

What kinds of devices are used to create effect?	Evidence	Effect on the reader
Contrast between humorous and serious situations.		
Hyperbole.		
Use of informal connectives.		

Some questions to help you revise the extract

1. See if you can find at least one example of the following in the extract and then explain its effect on the reader:

    - metaphor
    - the use of the senses
    - sentence structure that is used for effect.

2. What do you think were the author's reasons for writing this text? Remember that there can be more than one reason for writing a text – you started to explore this in the grid above, but can you think of any other motives?

3. Levine uses a single-sentence **paragraph** at the close of the piece – what is the effect of this?

Notes

A Passage to Africa (pages 20–25 in the student book)

- George Alagiah is a well-known and respected news correspondent for the BBC.

- He is from Sri Lanka but was brought up in West Africa before moving to the UK.

- This extract comes from his **autobiography**, *A Passage to Africa*, which is about his experiences as a correspondent in Africa. It tells the story of a report he made in Somalia.

- Somalia is in the east of Africa, east of Ethiopia, and this extract was written at a time of brutal civil war.

A Passage to Africa

I saw a thousand hungry, lean, scared and betrayed faces as I criss-crossed Somalia between the end of 1991 and December 1992, but there is one I will never forget.

I was in a little hamlet just outside Gufgaduud, a village in the back of beyond, a place the aid agencies had yet to reach. In my notebook I had jotted down instructions on how to get there. 'Take the Badale Road for a few kilometres till the end of the tarmac, turn right on to a dirt track, stay on it for about forty-five minutes – Gufgaduud. Go another fifteen minutes approx. – like a ghost village.'

10 In the ghoulish manner of journalists on the hunt for the most striking pictures, my cameraman and I tramped from one hut to another. What might have appalled us when we'd started our trip just a few days before no longer impressed us much. The search for the shocking is like the craving for a drug: you require heavier and more frequent doses the longer you're at it. Pictures that stun the editors one day are written off as the same old stuff the next. This sounds callous, but it is just a fact of life. It's how we collect and compile the images that so move people in the comfort of their sitting rooms back home.

There was Amina Abdirahman, who had gone out that morning in search
20 of wild, edible roots, leaving her two young girls lying on the dirt floor of their hut. They had been sick for days, and were reaching the final, enervating stages of terminal hunger. Habiba was ten years old and her sister, Ayaan, was nine. By the time Amina returned, she had only one daughter. Habiba had died. No rage, no whimpering, just a passing away – that simple, frictionless, motionless deliverance from a state of half-life to death itself. It was, as I said at the time in my dispatch, a vision of 'famine away from the headlines, a famine of quiet suffering and lonely death'.

There was the old woman who lay in her hut, abandoned by relations who were too weak to carry her on their journey to find food. It was the smell
30 that drew me to her doorway: the smell of decaying flesh. Where her shinbone should have been there was a festering wound the size of my hand. She'd been shot in the leg as the retreating army of the deposed dictator took revenge on whoever it found in its way. The shattered leg had fused into the gentle V-shape of a boomerang. It was rotting; she was rotting. You could see it in her sick, yellow eyes and smell it in the putrid air she recycled with every struggling breath she took.

And then there was the face I will never forget.

revulsion: disgust

My reaction to everyone else I met that day was a mixture of pity and revulsion*. Yes, revulsion. The degeneration of the human body, sucked of its natural vitality by the twin evils of hunger and disease, is a disgusting
40 thing. We never say so in our TV reports. It's a taboo that has yet to be breached. To be in a feeding centre is to hear and smell the excretion of fluids by people who are beyond controlling their bodily functions. To be in a feeding centre is surreptitiously* to wipe your hands on the back of your trousers after you've held the clammy palm of a mother who has just cleaned vomit from her child's mouth.

surreptitiously: secretly

There's pity, too, because even in this state of utter despair they aspire to a dignity that is almost impossible to achieve. An old woman will cover her shrivelled body with a soiled cloth as your gaze turns towards her. Or the old and dying man who keeps his hoe next to the mat with which, one day soon,
50 they will shroud his corpse, as if he means to go out and till the soil once all this is over.

I saw that face for only a few seconds, a fleeting meeting of eyes before the face turned away, as its owner retreated into the darkness of another hut. In those brief moments there had been a smile, not from me, but from the face. It was not a smile of greeting, it was not a smile of joy – how could it be? – but it was a smile nonetheless. It touched me in a way I could not explain. It moved me in a way that went beyond pity or revulsion.

What was it about that smile? I had to find out. I urged my translator to ask the man why he had smiled. He came back with an answer. 'It's just that he
60 was embarrassed to be found in this condition,' the translator explained. And then it clicked. That's what the smile had been about. It was the feeble smile that goes with apology, the kind of smile you might give if you felt you had done something wrong.

inured: hardened

Normally inured* to stories of suffering, accustomed to the evidence of deprivation, I was unsettled by this one smile in a way I had never been before. There is an unwritten code between the journalist and his subjects in these situations. The journalist observes, the subject is observed. The journalist is active, the subject is passive. But this smile had turned the tables on that tacit agreement. Without uttering a single word, the man had
70 posed a question that cut to the heart of the relationship between me and him, between us and them, between the rich world and the poor world. If he was embarrassed to be found weakened by hunger and ground down by conflict, how should I feel to be standing there so strong and confident?

I resolved there and then that I would write the story of Gufgaduud with all the power and purpose I could muster. It seemed at the time, and still does, the only adequate answer a reporter can give to the man's question.

I have one regret about that brief encounter in Gufgaduud. Having searched through my notes and studied the dispatch that the BBC broadcast, I see that I never found out what the man's name was. Yet
80 meeting him was a seminal moment in the gradual collection of experiences we call context. Facts and figures are the easy part of journalism. Knowing where they sit in the great scheme of things is much harder. So, my nameless friend, if you are still alive, I owe you one.

George Alagiah

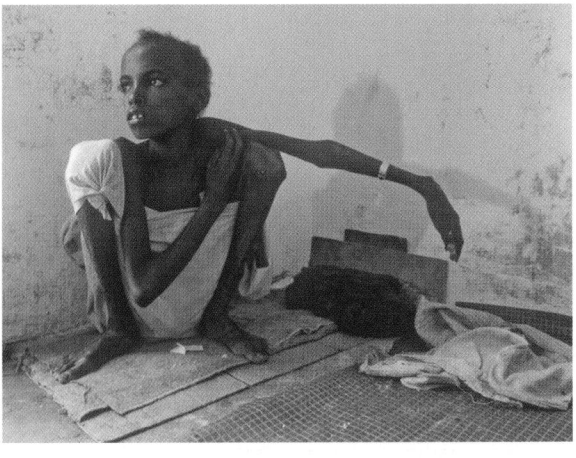

Points you may want to consider about this extract

- Autobiographies are written to retell stories from a personal point of view so there may be some bias in them.

- Alagiah wants to present the reader with a challenging experience here in order to make us think about how we consume the media reports we see.

A famine victim in Somalia, 1992.

Have a look at the tables below. The first suggests the intended purpose of the text, the second considers audience and the third discusses the techniques the author uses. You should copy and complete these tables and try to add to them yourself.

Purpose

Why has the text been written?	Evidence	Effect on the reader
		This description in the first sentence establishes what the extract will be about and that it will describe to us the suffering of the people Alagiah met.
To provoke a response from the reader.		

Audience

Who is the text aimed at?	Evidence	Effect on the reader
An adult audience.		
	'There was Amina Abdirahman...' and 'There was the old woman who lay in her hut...'	Alagiah retells the stories of the people he meets on his journey and gives us an insight into their lives. This would be interesting to those who want to learn about such things.

Techniques

What kinds of devices are used to create effect?	Evidence	Effect on the reader
Rhetorical question.		
Emotive vocabulary.		

Some questions to help you revise the extract

1. See if you can find at least one example of the following in the extract and then explain its effect on the reader:

   - distressing language

   - repetition

   - **simile**.

2. What do you think is the effect of the single-sentence paragraph?

3. What do you think Alagiah's motivations were for writing this piece?

4. What is the impact of the final sentence?

Notes

The Explorer's Daughter (pages 25–29 in the student book)

- Kari Herbert spent some of her childhood living in northwest Greenland in the Arctic.

- Her father was a polar explorer.

- This extract is taken from her book, which is partly autobiography and partly travelogue. Her book informs the reader about Greenland and its people, culture and animals.

- In this extract she recounts the story of a hunt for a narwhal – a type of whale.

- She is sympathetic to the hunters, who face terrible danger in the hunt, but is also sympathetic to the views of those who believe hunting is inhumane.

The Explorer's Daughter

Two hours after the last of the hunters had returned and eaten, narwhal were spotted again, this time very close. Within an hour even those of us on shore could with the naked eye see the plumes of spray from the narwhal catching the light in a spectral play of colour. Two large pods* of narwhal circled in the fjord*, often looking as if they were going to merge, but always slowly, methodically passing each other by. Scrambling back up to the lookout I looked across the glittering kingdom in front of me and took a sharp intake of breath. The hunters were dotted all around the fjord. The evening light was turning butter-gold, glinting off man and whale and

10 catching the soft billows of smoke from a lone hunter's pipe. From where we sat at the lookout it looked as though the hunters were close enough to touch the narwhal with their bare hands and yet they never moved. Distances are always deceptive in the Arctic, and I fell to wondering if the narwhal existed at all or were instead mischievous tricks of the shifting light.

pods: small groups of whales
fjord: a long, narrow inlet of the sea with steep sides

The narwhal rarely stray from High Arctic waters, escaping only to the slightly more temperate waters towards the Arctic Circle in the dead of winter, but never entering the warmer southern seas. In summer the hunters of Thule are fortunate to witness the annual return of the narwhal to the Inglefield Fjord, on the side of which we now sat.

20 The narwhal is an essential contributor to the survival of the hunters in the High Arctic. The mattak or blubber* of the whale is rich in necessary minerals and vitamins, and in a place where the climate prohibits the growth of vegetables or fruit, this rich source of vitamin C was the one reason that the Eskimos have never suffered from scurvy*. For centuries the blubber of the whales was also the only source of light and heat, and the dark rich meat is still a valuable part of the diet for both man and dogs (a single narwhal can feed a team of dogs for an entire month). Its single ivory tusk, which can grow up to six feet in length, was used for harpoon tips and handles for other hunting implements (although the

30 ivory was found to be brittle and not hugely satisfactory as a weapon), for carving protective tupilaks*, and even as a central beam for their small ancient dwellings. Strangely, the tusk seems to have little use for the narwhal itself; they do not use the tusk to break through ice as a breathing hole, nor will they use it to catch or attack prey, but rather the primary use seems to be to disturb the top of the sea bed in order to catch

mattak or blubber: the fatty skin of the whale

scurvy: a painful, weakening disease caused by lack of vitamin C

tupilaks: figures with magical powers, charms

predilection*: liking

Arctic halibut for which they have a particular predilection*. Often the ends of their tusks are worn down or even broken from such usage.

The women clustered on the knoll of the lookout, binoculars pointing in every direction, each woman focusing on her husband or family member, 40 occasionally spinning round at a small gasp or jump as one of the women saw a hunter near a narwhal. Each wife knew her husband instinctively and watched their progress intently; it was crucial to her that her husband catch a narwhal – it was part of their staple diet, and some of the mattak and meat could be sold to other hunters who hadn't been so lucky, bringing in some much-needed extra income. Every hunter was on the water. It was like watching a vast, waterborne game with the hunters spread like a net around the sound.

The narwhal are intelligent creatures, their senses are keen and they talk to one another under the water. Their hearing is particularly developed and 50 they can hear the sound of a paddling kayak from a great distance. That was why the hunters had to sit so very still in the water.

One hunter was almost on top of a pair of narwhal, and they were huge. He gently picked up his harpoon and aimed – in that split second my heart leapt for both hunter and narwhal. I urged the man on in my head; he was so close, and so brave to attempt what he was about to do – he was miles from land in a flimsy kayak, and could easily be capsized and drowned. The hunter had no rifle, only one harpoon with two heads and one bladder. It was a foolhardy exercise and one that could only inspire respect. And yet at the same time my heart also urged the narwhal to dive, to leave, to survive.

60 This dilemma stayed with me the whole time that I was in Greenland. I understand the harshness of life in the Arctic and the needs of the hunters and their families to hunt and live on animals and sea mammals that we demand to be protected because of their beauty. And I know that one

An Inughuit hunter harpoons a narwhal.

cannot afford to be sentimental in the Arctic. 'How can you possibly eat seal?' I have been asked over and over again. True, the images that bombarded us several years ago of men battering seals for their fur hasn't helped the issue of polar hunting, but the Inughuit do not kill seals using this method, nor do they kill for sport. They use every part of the animals they kill, and most of the food in Thule is still brought in by the hunter-

70 gatherers and fishermen. Imported goods can only ever account for part of the food supply; there is still only one annual supply ship that makes it through the ice to Qaanaaq, and the small twice-weekly plane from West Greenland can only carry a certain amount of goods. Hunting is still an absolute necessity in Thule.

Kari Herbert

Points you may want to consider about this extract

- As the author grew up in this environment, she clearly loves it and wants the reader to identify with that – this gives the writing a heavy bias.

- This writing is not just there to provide information; it is emotive as well.

Have a look at the tables below. The first suggests the intended purpose of the text, the second considers audience and the third discusses the techniques the author uses. You should copy and complete these tables and try to add to them yourself.

Purpose

Why has the text been written?	Evidence	Effect on the reader
To inform the reader about life in the Arctic Circle.	'The narwhal is an essential contributor to the survival of the hunters in the High Arctic... in a place where the climate prohibits growth of vegetables or fruit'.	

Audience

Who is the text aimed at?	Evidence	Effect on the reader
People with an interest in the world around them and how different cultures live.		

Techniques

What kinds of devices are used to create effect?	Evidence	Effect on the reader
Repeated imagery.		
Use of Inughuit vocabulary.		This lends the author a sense of authority on the topic as she understands the local language.
Simile.		

Some questions to help you revise the extract

1. What do you think are Herbert's reasons for writing this text?

2. See if you can find at least one example of the following in the extract and then explain its effect on the reader:

- metaphor

- punctuation used for effect

- opinions.

3. What is the effect of the sentence 'The evening light was turning butter-gold, glinting off man and whale and catching the soft billows of smoke from a lone hunter's pipe'? See if you can comment on the **imagery** that the author uses here.

Notes

Explorers, or Boys Messing About? Either Way, Taxpayer Gets Rescue Bill (pages 29–32 in the student book)

- This article was published in the *Guardian* newspaper in 2003.

- It tells the story of two young men rescued at sea by the Chilean Navy when their helicopter crashed in the Antarctic.

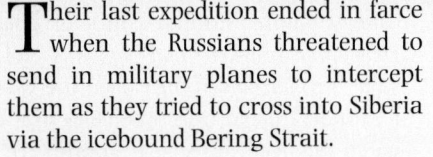

EXPLORERS, OR BOYS MESSING ABOUT?
EITHER WAY, TAXPAYER GETS RESCUE BILL

Their last expedition ended in farce when the Russians threatened to send in military planes to intercept them as they tried to cross into Siberia via the icebound Bering Strait.

Yesterday a new adventure undertaken by British explorers Steve Brooks and Quentin Smith almost led to tragedy when their helicopter plunged into the sea off Antarctica.

The men were plucked from the icy water by a Chilean naval ship after a nine-hour rescue which began when Mr Brooks contacted his wife, Jo Vestey, on his satellite phone asking for assistance. The rescue involved the Royal Navy, the RAF and British coastguards.

Last night there was resentment in some quarters that the men's adventure had cost the taxpayers of Britain and Chile tens of thousands of pounds.

Experts questioned the wisdom of taking a small helicopter – the four-seater Robinson R44 has a single engine – into such a hostile environment.

There was also confusion about what exactly the men were trying to achieve. A website set up to promote the Bering Strait expedition claims the team were planning to fly from the north to south pole in their 'trusty helicopter'.

But Ms Vestey claimed she did not know what the pair were up to, describing them as 'boys messing about with a helicopter'.

The drama began at around 1 am British time when Mr Brooks, 42, and 40-year-old Mr Smith, also known as Q, ditched into the sea 100 miles off

An icebreaker ship.

Antarctica, about 36 miles north of Smith Island, and scrambled into their liferaft.

Mr Brooks called his wife in London on his satellite phone. She said: 'He said they were both in the liferaft but were okay and could I call the emergency people?'

Meanwhile, distress signals were being beamed from the ditched helicopter and from Mr Brooks' Breitling emergency watch, a wedding present.

The signals from the aircraft were deciphered by Falmouth* coastguard and passed on to the rescue coordination centre at RAF Kinloss in Scotland.

The Royal Navy's ice patrol ship, HMS *Endurance*, which was 180 miles away surveying uncharted waters, began steaming towards the scene and dispatched its two Lynx helicopters.

One was driven back because of poor visibility but the second was on its way when the men were picked up by a Chilean naval vessel at about 10.20 am British time.

Falmouth*: coastal town in Cornwall, England

Though the pair wore survival suits and the weather at the spot where they ditched was clear, one Antarctic explor-
70 er told Mr Brooks' wife it was 'nothing short of a miracle' that they had survived.

Both men are experienced adventurers. Mr Brooks, a property developer from London, has taken part in expeditions to 70 countries in 15 years. He has trekked solo to Everest base camp and walked barefoot for three days in the Himalayas. He has negotiated the
80 white water rapids of the Zambezi river by kayak and survived a charge by a silverback gorilla in the Congo. He is also a qualified mechanical engineer and pilot.

He and his wife spent their honeymoon flying the helicopter from Alaska to Chile. The 16,000-mile trip took three months.

Mr Smith, also from London, claims
90 to have been flying since the age of five. He has twice flown a helicopter around the globe and won the world freestyle helicopter flying championship.

Despite their experience, it is not the first time they have hit the headlines for the wrong reasons.

In April, Mr Brooks and another explorer, Graham Stratford, were poised to become the first to complete a
100 crossing of the 56-mile wide frozen Bering Strait between the US and Russia in an amphibious vehicle, *Snowbird VI*, which could carve its way through ice floes and float in the water in between.

But they were forced to call a halt after the Russian authorities told them they would scramble military helicopters to lift them off the ice if they
110 crossed the border.

Ironically, one of the aims of the expedition, for which Mr Smith provided air back-up, was to demonstrate how good relations between East and West had become.

The wisdom of the team's latest adventure was questioned by, among others, Günter Endres, editor of *Jane's Helicopter Markets and Systems*, who
120 said: 'I'm surprised they used the R44. I wouldn't use a helicopter like that to go so far over the sea. It sounds as if they were pushing it to the maximum.'

A spokesman for the pair said it was not known what had gone wrong. The flying conditions had been 'excellent'.

The Ministry of Defence said the taxpayer would pick up the bill, as was normal in rescues in the UK and
130 abroad. The spokesperson said it was 'highly unlikely' it would recover any of the money.

Last night the men were on their way to the Chilean naval base Eduardo Frei, where HMS *Endurance* was to pick them up. Ms Vestey said: 'They have been checked and appear to be well. I don't know what will happen to them once they have been picked up by HMS
140 *Endurance* – they'll probably have their bottoms kicked and be sent home the long way.'

Steven Morris

Points you may want to consider about this extract

- Reporters have to bear in mind the bias of their newspaper and try to keep the content lively in order to sell more newspapers.

- The article comes from the *Guardian* newspaper, and newspapers tend to display bias.

Have a look at the tables on the following page. The first suggests the intended purpose of the text, the second considers audience and the third discusses the techniques the author uses. You should copy and complete these tables and try to add to them yourself.

Purpose

Why has the text been written?	Evidence	Effect on the reader
To inform the reader of the news story.		
To criticise the actions of the explorers.		

Audience

Who is the text aimed at?	Evidence	Effect on the reader
Readers of this newspaper.		
People who share the view of the author.		

Techniques

What kinds of devices are used to create effect?	Evidence	Effect on the reader
Sensationalised language.		

Some questions to help you revise the extract

1. What is the effect of the short paragraphs?

2. See if you can find at least one example of the following in the extract and then explain its effect on the reader:

- temporal connectives
- opinions presented as facts.

3. Explain the author's use of **irony** and sarcasm in the article and its effect on the reader.

Notes

Taking on the World (pages 33–36 in the student book)

- Dame Ellen MacArthur is a world-renowned yachtswoman.

- She broke the world records for a solo circumnavigation of the globe by a woman in 2001 and by anyone in 2005.

- This passage comes from her autobiography, *Taking on the World*, and tells the story of an attempt to repair her mast in terrible conditions during her solo voyage.

Taking on the World

mouse line*: length of wire wrapped across the mouth of a hook, or through a shackle pin and around the shackle, for the sake of security

halyard*: a rope used for raising and lowering sails

sheet*: a line to control the sails

reef*: reduces area of sails

jumar*: a climbing device that grips the rope so that it can be climbed

spreader*: a bar attached to a yacht's mast

I climbed the mast on Christmas Eve, and though I had time to get ready, it was the hardest climb to date. I had worked through the night preparing for it, making sure I had all the tools, mouse lines* and bits I might need, and had agonized for hours over how I should prepare the halyard* so that it would stream out easily below me and not get caught as I climbed.

When it got light I decided that the time was right. I kitted up in my middle-layer clothes as I didn't want to wear so much that I wouldn't be able to move freely up there. The most dangerous thing apart from falling off is to be thrown against the mast, and though I would be wearing a helmet it
10 would not be difficult to break bones up there.

I laid out the new halyard on deck, flaking it neatly so there were no twists. As I took the mast in my hands and began to climb I felt almost as if I was stepping on to the moon – a world over which I had no control. You can't ease the sheets* or take a reef*, nor can you alter the settings for the autopilot. If something goes wrong you are not there to attend to it. You are a passive observer looking down at your boat some 90 feet below you. After climbing just a couple of metres I realized how hard it was going to be, I couldn't feel my fingers – I'd need gloves, despite the loss in dexterity. I climbed down, getting soaked as we ploughed into a wave – the decks around my feet were
20 awash. I unclipped my jumar* from the halyard and put on a pair of sailing gloves. There would be no second climb on this one – I knew that I would not have the energy.

As I climbed my hands were more comfortable, and initially progress was positive. But it got harder and harder as I was not only pulling my own weight up as I climbed but also the increasingly heavy halyard – nearly 200 feet of rope by the time I made it to the top. The physical drain came far less from the climbing than from the clinging on. The hardest thing is just to hang on as the mast slices erratically through the air. There would be the odd massive wave which I could feel us surf down, knowing we would pile into the wave in front. I
30 would wrap my arms around the mast and press my face against its cold and slippery carbon surface, waiting for the shuddering slowdown. Eyes closed and teeth gritted, I hung on tight, wrists clenched together, and hoped. Occasionally on the smaller waves I would be thrown before I could hold on tight, and my body and the tools I carried were thrown away from the mast; I'd be hanging on by just one arm, trying to stop myself from smacking back into the rig.

By the third spreader* I was exhausted; the halyard was heavier and the motion more violent. I held on to her spreader base and hung there, holding tight to breathe more deeply and conjure up more energy. But I realized that

the halyard was tight and that it had caught on something. I knew that if I
40 went down to free it I would not have the energy to climb up once again. I
tugged and tugged on the rope – the frustration was unreal. It had to come,
quite simply the rope had to come free. Luckily with all the pulling I managed
to create enough slack to make it to the top, but now I was even more

exhausted. I squinted at the grey sky
above me and watched the mast-
head whip across the clouds. The
wind whistled past us, made visible
by the snow that had begun to fall.
Below the sea stretched out for ever,
50 the size and length of the waves
emphasized by this new aerial view.
This is what it must look like to the
albatross.

  I rallied once more and left the
safety of the final spreader for my
last hike to the top. The motion was
worse than ever, and as I climbed I
thought to myself, not far now,
kiddo, come on, just keep moving...
60 As the mast-head came within reach
there was a short moment of relief;
at least there was no giving up now I
had made it – whatever happened
now I had the whole mast to climb

Ellen MacArthur.

down. I fumbled at the top of the rig, feeding in the halyard and connecting
the other end to the top of *Kingfisher*'s mast. The job only took half an hour
– then I began my descent. This was by far the most dangerous part and I
had my heart in my mouth – no time for complacency now, I thought, not
till you reach the deck, kiddo, it's far from over...
70 It was almost four hours before I called Mark back and I shook with
exhaustion as we spoke. We had been surfing at well over 20 knots while I
was up there. My limbs were bruised and my head was spinning, but I felt
like a million dollars as I spoke on the phone. Santa had called on *Kingfisher*
early and we had the best present ever – a new halyard.

Ellen MacArthur

Points you may want to consider about this extract

- Dame Ellen MacArthur is a well-known figure and so some people may have preconceived ideas about the challenges she has faced.

- Consider how MacArthur uses language to create a sense of tension here – look at the contrast between the technical and the emotive language.

Have a look at the tables on the following page. The first suggests the intended purpose of the text, the second considers audience and the third discusses the techniques the author uses. You should copy and complete these tables and try to add to them yourself.

Purpose

Why has the text been written?	Evidence	Effect on the reader
To inform the reader of MacArthur's struggles.		
To entertain the reader.	'Eyes closed and teeth gritted, I hung on tight, wrists clenched together, and hoped.'	

Audience

Who is the text aimed at?	Evidence	Effect on the reader
Yachting enthusiasts.		

Techniques

What kinds of devices are used to create effect?	Evidence	Effect on the reader
Simple sentences.		
Simile.		This allows the reader to imagine the feelings of the writer and to better identify with her.
	'you'.	This places the reader directly at the centre of the action.
Colloquialism.		

Some questions to help you revise the extract

1. Why does MacArthur occasionally use the **second-person** pronoun 'you'?

2. Is this text just for those interested in sailing? Explain your answer with examples from the text.

3. See if you can find at least one example of the following in the extract and then explain its effect on the reader:

- metaphor
- punctuation used for effect
- repetition.

4. What is the effect of using the sailing **jargon**?

Notes

Chinese Cinderella (pages 37–42 in the student book)

- Adeline Yen Mah grew up in Hong Kong in the 1950s.
- *Chinese Cinderella* tells the story of her childhood in her wealthy but dysfunctional family.
- It is an example of autobiographical writing.

Adeline Yen Mah.

Chinese Cinderella

Time went by relentlessly and it was Saturday again. Eight weeks more and it would be the end of term... in my case perhaps the end of school forever.

Four of us were playing Monopoly. My heart was not in it and I was losing steadily. Outside it was hot and there was a warm wind blowing. The radio warned of a possible typhoon the next day. It was my turn and I threw the dice. As I played, the thought of leaving school throbbed at the back of my mind like a persistent toothache.

'Adeline!' Ma-mien Valentino was calling.

'You can't go now,' Mary protested. 'For once I'm winning. One, two, three,
10 four. Good! You've landed on my property. Thirty-five dollars, please. Oh, good afternoon, Mother Valentino!'

We all stood up and greeted her.

'Adeline, didn't you hear me call you? Hurry up downstairs! Your chauffeur is waiting to take you home!'

Full of foreboding, I ran downstairs as in a nightmare, wondering who had died this time. Father's chauffeur assured me everyone was healthy.

'Then why are you taking me home?' I asked.

'How should *I* know?' he answered defensively, shrugging his shoulders. 'Your guess is as good as mine. They give the orders and I carry them out.'

20 During the short drive home, my heart was full of dread and I wondered what I had done wrong. Our car stopped at an elegant villa at mid-level, halfway up the hill between the peak and the harbour.

'Where are we?' I asked foolishly.

'Don't you know anything?' the chauffeur replied rudely. 'This is your new home. Your parents moved here a few months ago.'

'I had forgotten,' I said as I got out.

Ah Gum opened the door. Inside, it was quiet and cool.

'Where is everyone?'

'Your mother is out playing bridge. Your two brothers and Little Sister are
30 sunbathing by the swimming-pool. Your father is in his room and wants to see you as soon as you get home.'

'See me in his room?' I was overwhelmed by the thought that I had been summoned by Father to enter the Holy of Holies – a place to which I had never been invited. Why?

Timidly, I knocked on the door. Father was alone, looking relaxed in his slippers and bathrobe, reading a newspaper. He smiled as I entered and I saw he was in a happy mood. I breathed a small sigh of relief at first but became uneasy when I wondered why he was being so nice, thinking, *Is this a giant ruse on his part to trick me? Dare I let my guard down?*

40 'Sit down! Sit down!' He pointed to a chair. 'Don't look so scared. Here, take a look at this! They're writing about someone we both know, I think.'

He handed me the day's newspaper and there, in one corner, I saw my name ADELINE YEN in capital letters prominently displayed.

'It was announced today that 14-year-old Hong Kong schoolgirl ADELINE JUN-LING YEN of Sacred Heart Canossian School, Caine Road, Hong Kong, has won first prize in the International Play-writing Competition held in London, England, for the 1951–1952 school year. It is the first time that any local Chinese student from Hong Kong has won such a prestigious event. Besides a medal, the prize comes with a cash reward of FIFTY ENGLISH
50 POUNDS. Our sincere congratulations, ADELINE YEN, for bringing honour to Hong Kong. We are proud of you.'

Is it possible? Am I dreaming? Me, the winner?

'I was going up the lift this morning with my friend C.Y. Tung when he showed me this article and asked me, "Is the winner Adeline Jun-ling Yen related to you? The two of you have the same uncommon last name." Now C.Y. himself has a few children about your age but so far none of them has won an international literary prize, as far as I know. So I was quite pleased to tell him you are my daughter. Well done!'

He looked radiant. For once, he was proud of me. In front of his revered
60 colleague, C.Y. Tung, a prominent fellow businessman also from Shanghai, I had given him face. I thought, *Is this the big moment I have been waiting for? My whole being vibrated with all the joy in the world. I only had to stretch out my hand to reach the stars.*

'Tell me, how did you do it?' he continued. 'How come *you* won?'

'Well, the rules and regulations were so very complicated. One really has to be dedicated just to understand what they want. Perhaps I was the only one determined enough to enter and there were no other competitors!'

He laughed approvingly. 'I doubt it very much but that's a good answer.'

'Please, Father,' I asked boldly, thinking it was now or never. 'May I go to
70 university in England too, just like my brothers?'

'I do believe you have potential. Tell me, what would you study?'

My heart gave a giant lurch as it dawned on me that he was agreeing to let me go. How marvellous it was simply to be alive! Study? I thought. Going to England is like entering heaven. Does it matter what you do after you get to heaven?

But Father was expecting an answer. What about creative writing? After all, I had just won first prize in an international writing competition!

'I plan to study literature. I'll be a writer.'

'Writer!' he scoffed. 'You are going to starve! What language are you going to
80 write in and who is going to read your writing? Though you may think you're
an expert in both Chinese and English, your Chinese is actually rather
elementary. As for your English, don't you think the native English speakers
can write better than you?'

I waited in silence. I did not wish to contradict him.

'You will go to England with Third Brother this summer and you will go to medical
school. After you graduate, you will specialise in obstetrics*. Women will always
be having babies. Women patients prefer women doctors. You will learn to deliver
their babies. That's a foolproof profession for you. Don't you agree?'

> obstetrics*: caring for
> women who are having
> babies

Agree? Of course I agreed. Apparently, he had it all planned out. As long as he
90 let me go to university in England, I would study anything he wished. How did
that line go in Wordsworth's poem? *Bliss was it in that dawn to be alive.*

'Father, I shall go to medical school in England and become a doctor. Thank
you very, very much.'

Adeline Yen Mah

Points you may want to consider about this extract

- This work is written as a memoir, which means that the author is looking back from later in life – this may change the slant or bias of the writing.

- Sometimes in autobiographical writing the details or conversations are changed to make it more emotive, more engaging or more entertaining.

- This passage is not only about Adeline Yen Mah herself but also about her relationship with her family.

Have a look at the tables below. The first suggests the intended purpose of the text, the second considers audience and the third discusses the techniques the author uses. You should copy and complete these tables and try to add to them yourself.

Purpose

Why has the text been written?	Evidence	Effect on the reader
To inform the reader of what it was like in Yen Mah's family.		

Audience

Who is the text aimed at?	Evidence	Effect on the reader

Techniques

What kinds of devices are used to create effect?	Evidence	Effect on the reader
Ellipses.	'... the end of term... in my case perhaps the end of school forever.'	
		The descriptive power of this simile establishes how uncomfortable the author was with the idea of leaving school.
Change of tense from past to present.		
Metaphor.		

Some questions to help you revise the extract

1. Why do you think that Yen Mah refers to her father's study as the 'Holy of Holies'? What effect does this have on the reader?

2. What do you think Yen Mah's reason for writing this autobiography was?

3. How does Yen Mah create a sense of her culture in this extract?

4. See if you can find at least one example of the following in the extract and then explain its effect on the reader:

- simile
- **rhetorical question**
- punctuation used for effect.

Notes

Chapter 2: Section B Anthology Texts

Introduction

In this section of the revision guide we will look at each of the Section B anthology texts for both specifications. Just as for the Section A anthology texts, you will be expected to explore the extracts and demonstrate your own insights. For each extract in this section we will focus on the same three ideas related to the assessment objectives:

- meaning
- language devices
- structural devices.

You should try to add to these with your own ideas.

Know your assessment objective

As in Section A, in this part of the exam you will be demonstrating that you can achieve the objectives set out below. On the left are the assessment objectives and on the right there are interpretations of each aspect.

AO2 (i): Read and understand texts with insight and engagement.	Demonstrate that you *understand* the text, and can use *quotations* and references to show that you have formed your own *interesting ideas* about it.
AO2 (ii): Develop and sustain interpretations of writers' ideas and perspectives.	Show that you understand what the writer is trying to communicate and show that you know what is *reality* and what are the writer's *feelings*.
AO2 (iii): Understand and make some evaluation of how writers use linguistic and structural devices to achieve their effects.	Discuss how *effective writers' choices* are on a *word, sentence and text level* in creating a desired *effect*.

What the examiner wants

You need to be able to communicate to the examiner that you can fulfil the brief of the assessment objectives. There are several ways that you can ensure you do this. The examiner wants to see:

- clear, concise answers that fully address the question
- answers that meet the needs of the question – a three-mark question does not demand a whole essay as an answer (the number of lines in the answer booklet of your exam paper should be a good guide)
- a clear understanding of the text
- a specific focus on language and structural techniques that create effect
- quotations from the text that are appropriate for the answer you give.

Disabled (pages 43–46 in the student book)

- Wilfred Owen was a poet who lived from 1893 to 1918 and died just seven days before the end of World War I.
- He fought in the British Army throughout the war but spent some time during the war in a hospital called Craiglockhart.
- At Craiglockhart, he met other soldiers who also expressed themselves through poetry – most notably Siegfried Sassoon.

Meaning: What is the text about?

Read the poem through and jot down what you think it is about. What is the 'story' or **narrative** of the poem and what do you think Owen was trying to communicate to us?

Nameless – he may be seen as representative of all soldiers.

Does this refer to the suit or the man?

'Colour' is a euphemism for blood – he can't refer to it directly.

'Race' implies some kind of fun or competition.

This is ironic if you consider his current state.

Semi-colon represents his pause for thought.

This is almost a direct address to the reader.

Disabled

He sat in a wheeled chair, waiting for dark,
And shivered in his ghastly suit of grey,
Legless, sewn short at elbow. Through the park
Voices of boys rang saddening like a hymn,
5 Voices of play and pleasure after day,
Till gathering sleep had mothered them from him.

About this time Town used to swing so gay
When glow-lamps budded in the light blue trees,
And girls glanced lovelier as the air grew dim, –
10 In the old times, before he threw away his knees.
Now he will never feel again how slim
Girls' waists are, or how warm their subtle hands,
All of them touch him like some queer disease.

There was an artist silly for his face,
15 For it was younger than his youth, last year.
Now, he is old; his back will never brace;
He's lost his colour very far from here,
Poured it down shell-holes till the veins ran dry,
And half his lifetime lapsed in the hot race
20 And leap of purple spurted from his thigh.

One time he liked a blood-smear down his leg,
After the matches, carried shoulder-high.
It was after football, when he'd drunk a peg,
He thought he'd better join. – He wonders why.
25 Someone had said he'd look a god in kilts.
That's why; and maybe, too, to please his Meg,
Aye, that was it, to please the giddy jilts
He asked to join. He didn't have to beg;

Smiling they wrote his lie: aged nineteen years.
30 Germans he scarcely thought of; all their guilt,
And Austria's, did not move him. And no fears
Of Fear came yet. He thought of jewelled hilts
For daggers in plaid socks; of smart salutes;
And care of arms; and leave; and pay arrears;
35 *Esprit de corps*; and hints for young recruits.
And soon, he was drafted out with drums and cheers.

Some cheered him home, but not as crowds cheer Goal.
Only a solemn man who brought him fruits
Thanked him; and then inquired about his soul.

40 Now, he will spend a few sick years in institutes,
And do what things the rules consider wise,
And take whatever pity they may dole.
Tonight he noticed how the women's eyes
Passed from him to the strong men that were whole.
45 How cold and late it is! Why don't they come
And put him into bed? Why don't they come?

> Use of enjambment means that the true meaning isn't revealed until the second line – it is fear that the soldiers are scared of.
>
> List of short phrases separated by semi-colons represents his excitement.
>
> At the end of the poem he is left completely isolated and alone.

Some activities to help you revise the text

1. The annotated version of the poem shows you some of the comments you may want to make about language, structure and meaning. See if you can add your own by answering the following questions about the text:

- Comment on the imagery in the poem and how this imagery is created.

- Explain the use of the following devices in the poem, giving examples: Repetition, **personification**, **alliteration**, metaphor.

- Look at the structure of the poem. Why do you think there is a stanza that is shorter than the others?

- Look at the punctuation used by the poet. What do the dashes in lines 9 and 24 represent? What do the italics in line 39 mean?

2. Much of the meaning of the poem is revealed through the contrast between how the soldier saw himself before he lost his limbs and how he sees himself after. Select two phrases, one that represents the soldier's frame of mind before and one that represents his frame of mind after.

3. What do you think is the impact of the final two lines of the poem?

4. Which stanza is the most important and why?

5. Why do you think Owen chose not to give his soldier a name?

Red Cross workers in a trench tending to a wounded soldier, 1918.

6. Have a look at the student's writing below – this is an excerpt from their exam answer in which they are writing about language devices. See if you can decide which parts of the answer each examiner comment refers to.

How does Owen try to bring out the sadness of the soldier in the poem? You must consider:

- the context of the poem
- the language Owen uses
- the structural devices.

You should refer closely to the poem to support your answer. You may use brief quotations.

15 marks (24 marks for Certificate students)

Student answer

Owen's work is full of linguistic devices which give the reader a sense of how the soldier feels about himself now that he has lost his limbs. In the very first stanza, a clear image of sadness pervades as words like '... dark... shivered... grey...' create a sense of cold and isolation. Further to this, Owen uses repetition at the beginning of lines 4 and 5 where the 'Voices of boys...' and the 'Voices of play...' emphasise how alone and sad the soldier is – he is so far from this kind of joy that he may never regain it. In the final line of the stanza the word 'mothered' is used to show how these boys have someone to look after and care for them, while the soldier is alone, foretelling the events of the final lines, when no one comes to help him into bed.

Examiner's comments:

- clear reference to language devices is supported by evidence and explanation – demonstrates insight
- good evaluation of the effect of the language devices and linking to good knowledge of the poem
- could be clearer
- links are made between the effect of the language devices and how these create meaning.

Notes

Out, Out – (pages 47–50 in the student book)

> - Robert Frost is regarded as one of the most important American poets of the 20th century.
> - His poems often focus on pastoral life in New England.

A young boy using farm machinery in America, 1916.

Meaning: What is the text about?

First of all, consider the narrative of the poem – what is the story being told? Next, think about the meaning behind the story – what is the poet trying to tell us about life and humanity?

Out, Out –

The buzz saw snarled and rattled in the yard
And made dust and dropped stove-length sticks of wood,
Sweet-scented stuff when the breeze drew across it.
And from there those that lifted eyes could count
5 Five mountain ranges one behind the other
Under the sunset far into Vermont.
And the saw snarled and rattled, snarled and rattled,
As it ran light, or had to bear a load.
And nothing happened: Day was all but done.
10 Call it a day, I wish they might have said
To please the boy by giving him the half hour
That a boy counts so much when saved from work.
His sister stood beside him in her apron
To tell them 'Supper.' At the word, the saw,
15 As if to prove saws knew what supper meant,
Leaped out at the boy's hand, or seemed to leap –
He must have given the hand. However it was,
Neither refused the meeting. But the hand!
The boy's first outcry was a rueful laugh,
20 As he swung toward them holding up the hand,
Half in appeal, but half as if to keep
The life from spilling. Then the boy saw all–
Since he was old enough to know, big boy
Doing a man's work, though a child at heart–
25 He saw all spoiled. 'Don't let him cut my hand off–
The doctor, when he comes. Don't let him, sister!'
So. But the hand was gone already.
The doctor put him in the dark of ether.
He lay and puffed his lips out with his breath.
30 And then–the watcher at his pulse took fright.
No one believed. They listened at his heart.
Little–less–nothing!–and that ended it.
No more to build on there. And they, since they
Were not the one dead, turned to their affairs.

Annotations:

Reference to a line in *Macbeth* ('out, out brief candle') that refers to how short life is.

Alliteration reflects the sound of the saw.

Use of colon – perhaps represents day drawing to a close.

Unknown narrator – is this the poet's view?

Simple sentence punctuated with an exclamation mark shows us the result of the accident.

Childish phrasing reminds us that this poem is about a child.

The other characters return immediately to work.

Some activities to help you revise the text

1. The annotated version of the poem shows you some of the comments you may want to make about language, structure and meaning. See if you can add your own by answering the following questions about the text:

- Find an example of each of the following and comment on what effect the poet creates by using them: Personification, **onomatopoeia**, metaphor.

- What do you think the reduction in the length of phrases and sentences represents towards the end of the poem?

- What effect does the repetition of 'the saw snarled and rattled' create?

2. What do you think is the reason that Frost told this story? What was his motive?

3. Why do you think Frost chose to make it a single-stanza poem?

4. Why does Frost mention the 'Five mountain ranges one behind the other'?

5. The following three students make the same point about the poem in their exams – which one do you think does it best and why?

Student A

Frost uses a range of different sentence structures to create a sense of the passage of time in this poem. He uses long ones when describing the scene and then short ones when the action starts to happen. This is because he wanted to make it exciting and tense for the reader.

Student B

Frost has employed several different sentence structures throughout the piece to create a sense of the drama of the accident. At the beginning of the poem sentences are long and descriptive:

'The buzz saw snarled and rattled... Vermont.'

There is a sense that the poet can take his time and set the scene. However, once the accident takes place the sentences and phrases become short and disjointed as though Frost is in a rush to complete the story before the boy's time runs out:

'So. But the hand was gone already... Little – less – nothing!'

Student C

Robert uses a range of different sentence structures to create a sense of the passage of time in this poem. He uses long ones when describing the scene, like the opening sentence of the poem, which shows us the setting and the countryside, and then short ones when the action starts to happen such as 'So.' This creates a build up in the tension of the poem for the reader and keeps us on the edge of our seats.

TOP TIP ✓

Avoid phrases such as 'on the edge of our seat' – this is colloquial and does not really mean anything. Instead say that the text 'emphasises', 'supports' or 'demonstrates' something.

Refugee Blues (pages 51–53 in the student book)

- W.H. Auden (1907–1973) was an English poet.
- He is well known for his political views and powerful poetry.
- He was born and brought up in England but moved to America in 1939.
- He was a fan of blues music.
- This poem was written before the outbreak of World War II in 1939.

Jewish refugees queue up outside a reception centre after their arrival from Poland.

Meaning: What is the poem about?

After you have read the poem through, see if you can make some notes on what you think it is about.

Refugee Blues

Say this city has ten million souls,
Some are living in mansions, some are living in holes:
Yet there's no place for us, my dear, yet there's no place for us.

Once we had a country and we thought it fair,
5 Look in the atlas and you'll find it there:
We cannot go there now, my dear, we cannot go there now.

In the village churchyard there grows an old yew,
Every spring it blossoms anew:
Old passports can't do that, my dear, old passports can't do that.

10 The consul banged the table and said:
'If you've got no passport you're officially dead':
But we are still alive, my dear, but we are still alive.

Went to a committee; they offered me a chair;
Asked me politely to return next year:
15 But where shall we go to-day, my dear, but where shall we go to-day?

Came to a public meeting; the speaker got up and said:
'If we let them in, they will steal our daily bread';
He was talking of you and me, my dear, he was talking of you and me.

Thought I heard the thunder rumbling in the sky;
20 It was Hitler over Europe, saying: 'They must die';
We were in his mind, my dear, we were in his mind.

Saw a poodle in a jacket fastened with a pin,
Saw a door opened and a cat let in:
But they weren't German Jews, my dear, but they weren't German Jews.

> They cannot even find a 'hole' to live in.
>
> 'Fair' could mean 'equal' or 'beautiful'.
>
> Colon represents the finality of the consul's decision.

25 Went down the harbour and stood upon the quay,
Saw the fish swimming as if they were free:
Only ten feet away, my dear, only ten feet away.

Walked through a wood, saw the birds in the trees;
They had no politicians and sang at their ease:
30 They weren't the human race, my dear, they weren't the human race.

Dreamed I saw a building with a thousand floors,
A thousand windows and a thousand doors;
Not one of them was ours, my dear, not one of them was ours.

Stood on a great plain in the falling snow;
35 Ten thousand soldiers marched to and fro:
Looking for you and me, my dear, looking for you and me.

> Dream-like quality shows the nightmarish conditions of life for the refugees and also tells of the horrors of war.

Some activities to help you revise the text

1. The annotated version of the poem shows you some of the comments you may want to make about language, structure and meaning. See if you can add your own by answering the following questions about the text:

- What do you think the simple rhyme structure implies?

- Explain the use of juxtaposition in this poem, with examples.

- Comment on the use of metaphor and analogy in this poem, with examples.

- How is the state portrayed in the poem? Give examples.

2. Who do you think is the speaker and who is being spoken to? Why?

3. Why do you think Auden chose to structure the poem as a blues song?

4. The poem uses quite **informal** phrasing and often leaves out the pronoun 'I' – why do you think the poet may have chosen to write like this?

Notes

An Unknown Girl (pages 54–57 in the student book)

- Moniza Alvi is a poet and writer of Pakistani and English descent.
- She was born in Pakistan but brought up in England and her writing is often concerned with the relationship between Eastern and Western cultures.

Meaning: What is the poem about?

Read the poem through again and think about what it is about. Is it just the story of the poet having her hands hennaed or is there a deeper meaning?

An Unknown Girl

In the evening bazaar
    studded with neon
        an unknown girl
    is hennaing my hand.
5   She squeezes a wet brown line
        from a nozzle.
        She is icing my hand,
    which she steadies with hers
        on her satin-peach knee.
10   In the evening bazaar
        for a few rupees
        an unknown girl
    is hennaing my hand.
    As a little air catches
15 my shadow-stitched kameez
        a peacock spreads its lines
        across my palm.
    Colours leave the street
        float up in balloons.
20 Dummies in shop-fronts
        tilt and stare
    with their Western perms.
    Banners for Miss India 1993,
        for curtain cloth
25   and sofa cloth
        canopy me.
    I have new brown veins.
    In the evening bazaar
        very deftly
30   an unknown girl

'Neon' could represent modernity creeping into an ancient place.

'Icing' gives the impression of decoration.

May imply the 'darkness' or hidden nature of the other culture that Alvi represents.

Metaphor for darkness falling – perhaps suggesting a carnival spirit.

Word choice makes the dummies seem ridiculous and fake and perhaps the Western culture along with them.

Metaphor for India becoming part of her, as though the henna is transforming her from the inside.

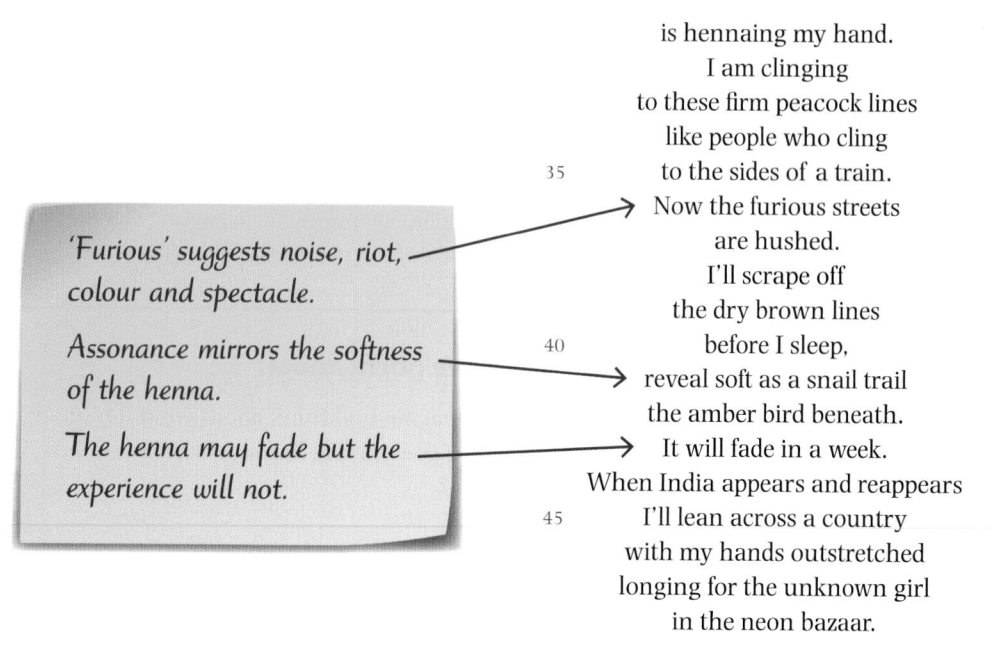

is hennaing my hand.
I am clinging
to these firm peacock lines
like people who cling
35   to the sides of a train.
Now the furious streets
are hushed.
I'll scrape off
the dry brown lines
40   before I sleep,
reveal soft as a snail trail
the amber bird beneath.
It will fade in a week.
When India appears and reappears
45   I'll lean across a country
with my hands outstretched
longing for the unknown girl
in the neon bazaar.

'Furious' suggests noise, riot, colour and spectacle.

Assonance mirrors the softness of the henna.

The henna may fade but the experience will not.

Some activities to help you revise the text

1. The annotated version of the poem shows you some of the comments you may want to make about language, structure and meaning. See if you can add your own by answering the following questions about the text:

   • The poem is written in free verse – what do you think this form might represent?

   • Comment on the imagery in the poem and how this imagery is created.

   • What effect is created by the repetition of the line 'In the evening bazaar'?

   • Comment on the simile used in lines 32–35.

   • What do you think the metaphor in the last five lines of the poem represents?

2. Try to create a list of words in the poem that might represent Eastern culture to the speaker of the poem and a list of words that might represent Western culture.

3. What is the importance of the girl being unknown?

4. Consider the use of colour imagery in the poem – what impact do you think it might have on the reader?

Notes

Electricity Comes to Cocoa Bottom (pages 58–61 in the student book)

- Marcia Douglas was born in the UK to Jamaican parents in 1961.
- She moved to Jamaica as a child and grew up in a rural area there.
- She left Jamaica to study for her Masters degree and her PhD in 1990.
- Her work has received many awards and nominations.

Meaning: What is the poem about?

After you have read the poem through again, make some notes on what you think it is about. Why do you think Douglas wants to tell this story?

Electricity Comes to Cocoa Bottom

Then all the children of Cocoa Bottom
went to see Mr. Samuel's electric lights.
They camped on the grass bank outside his house,
their lamps filled with oil,
5   waiting for sunset,
watching the sky turn yellow, orange. ←

> The colours of the traditional oil lighting – perhaps also colours we associate with warm climates?

Grannie Patterson across the road
peeped through the crack in her porch door.
The cable was drawn like a pencil line across the sun.
10 The fireflies waited in the shadows,
their lanterns off.
The kling-klings swooped in from the hills,
congregating in the orange trees.
A breeze coming home from sea held its breath;
15 bamboo lining the dirt road stopped its swaying,
and evening came as soft as chiffon curtains:
Closing. Closing.

Light!
Mr. Samuel smiling on the verandah –
20 a silhouette against the yellow shimmer behind him – ←
and there arising such a gasp,
such a fluttering of wings,
tweet-a-whit,
such a swaying, swaying. ←
25 Light! Marvellous light!
And then the breeze rose up from above the trees,
swelling and swelling into a wind
such that the long grass bent forward
stretching across the bank like so many bowed heads. ←
30 And a voice in the wind whispered:
Is there one among us to record this moment?
But there was none –

> Imagery makes Mr. Samuel almost God-like as he commands electricity.

> Repetition suggests the rhythms of nature as untouched by the coming developments of electricity.

> This simile, however, suggests nature must give way to progress.

no one (except for a few warm rocks
hidden among mongoose ferns) even heard a sound.
35 Already the children of Cocoa Bottom
had lit their lamps for the dark journey home,
and it was too late –
the moment had passed.

Short final stanza may suggest the anti-climax as everyone has already left the scene.

Some activities to help you revise the text

1. The annotated version of the poem shows you some of the comments you may want to make about language, structure and meaning. See if you can add your own by answering the following questions about the text:

   - What effect does the repetition in line 17 create? What effect does the repetition of 'Light!' create?

   - What do you think the simile in line 9 represents?

   - What tense is used in line 36 and what effect does it create?

2. Why do you think the poet chose to start the poem with the word 'Then...'?

3. Create a list of all the natural imagery in the poem – what is the significance of this imagery?

4. The use of many close-packed verbs in this poem gives the text a sense of movement – see if you can highlight all of the verbs.

Notes

The Last Night (from *Charlotte Gray*) (pages 62–66 in the student book)

- This extract comes from a novel by Sebastian Faulks, a well-known contemporary novelist.
- The novel *Charlotte Gray* is the story of a Scottish woman who joins the French resistance to fight against the Nazis.
- It was written in 1999.

Meaning: What is the text about?

Read the extract over to refresh it in your mind. What is the text about? Who are the protagonists and what is the point that Faulks is making?

Here are some notes on the language and structure of the text.

Language

- The juxtaposition of 'sobbing passion' and 'punctilious care' in line 6 highlights the very different responses to trauma.

- Lines 14–15: Image of natural beauty, youth and colour amid the despair.

Jews in Warsaw waiting for deportation to a concentration camp.

- The word choices in paragraphs three to five – 'small hours of the night', 'low part of the night', 'deepest moments of their sleep' – are contrasted with the activity and intrusion into the quiet night from paragraph seven onwards, with paragraph six acting as a bridge.

Structure

- Lines 36–38: The short paragraph could suggest the speed with which the children were removed.

- Lines 47–48: The short clause implies the finality of the moment.

Some activities to help you revise the text

1. Look at the notes on the text above and try to add to them, thinking about the linguistic and structural devices used by the author and the effects they create.

2. Explain the language device used in lines 30–31. What is the image created similar to?

3. Part of what makes this such an effective piece of writing is the wide array of emotions that are expressed. See if you can highlight all the words associated with emotions and add a comment to each – what is the effect that the author intended?

4. We are shown a snapshot of a mother as she watches her child taken onto the bus for transportation to the concentration camp. How does Faulks use language to make this a powerful part of the extract?

5. Two students attempted to answer question 4. Which one gives the better response and why?

Student A

Faulks uses language to create a very emotive picture of the woman as she watches her child leave. The words 'terrible ferocity' give us a sense of the strength of the mother's love – it is almost primal in its intensity. The fact that the little boy who witnesses the look confuses it with hatred intensifies the image and the use of a rhetorical question makes us question her in the same way.

Student B

Faulks uses language to create a very emotive picture of the woman as she watches her child leave. Her look is one of 'terrible ferocity' and she is trying to 'remember, for ever'. Andre realises she wants to 'fix the picture... in her mind' and mistakes the look for hate.

6. Now take student B's answer and see if you can improve it – think carefully about the extract and about what the examiner is looking for.

Notes

Veronica (pages 67–73 in the student book)

- Adewale Maja-Pearce is a Nigerian author who grew up in Lagos, Nigeria, but was educated in London.
- Much of his writing is concerned with his experiences in Nigeria.
- Nigeria has a troubled history involving bloody civil war and struggles for power.

Meaning: What is the text about?

Read the extract over once again and think about what it is about. While it is a straightforward story, what do you think that the author was trying to communicate about life in this place and at this time?

Here are some notes on the language and structure of the text.

Language

- 'I thought I knew my own worth' in line 21 suggests the wisdom of hindsight.
- The informal connective ('well') in line 54 gives the story a personal feel.

Structure

- The long sentence in lines 14–17 and the repetition of 'and' reinforce the idea of Veronica's questions being 'endless'.
- The long passages of direct speech allow us to catch up quickly with what has happened to the characters over time and keep pace in the story.

Some activities to help you revise the text

1. Look at the notes on the text above and try to add to them, thinking about the linguistic and structural devices used by the author and the effects they create.

2. What might the repeated imagery of the stream throughout the passage represent?

3. This story explores the life of a village in Nigeria. See if you can find some phrases that Maja-Pearce uses to establish what life is like in this village.

4. How does the representation of village life contrast with that of city life?

5. How would you describe Okeke? Use some quotations to back up your answer.

6. What kind of person is Veronica? Again, use evidence from the text to support your ideas.

7. Why does Veronica die at the end? How would the story have affected you if she had lived?

The Necklace (pages 73–83 in the student book)

- Guy de Maupassant (1850–1893) was a very influential French writer of short stories.
- This story has been translated from the original French in which it was published.
- In the latter half of the 19th century, France was divided by a rigid class structure.

Guy de Maupassant.

Meaning: What is the text about?

Once you've read over the text, it should be straightforward to explain the narrative. However, have you thought about the moral of the story? What was de Maupassant trying to teach us?

Here are some notes on the language and structure of the text.

Language

- The use of the word 'tribe' in line 201 suggests that the moneylenders are primitive and function together in an almost animalistic way.

- In lines 140–141, Monsieur Loisel uses informal **slang** ('Wait a sec'), which suggests he does not have the same pretentions as his wife.

- In line 122, the use of the word 'treasure' might suggest Madame Loisel is making off with something she has found and emphasises the perceived value of the necklace.

Structure

- Long paragraphs are used at the beginning of the extract to set the scene and repetition is used to help the reader understand Madame Loisel's circumstances and what she hopes for in the future.

- Three single-sentence paragraphs in lines 226–230 are used to emphasise the barren sparseness of the couple's new lifestyle.

Some activities to help you revise the text

1. Look at the notes on the text above and try to add to them, thinking about the linguistic and structural devices used by the author and the effects they create.

2. Give an example of a triplet (list of three things) and explain its effect.

3. What effect does the ending have on the reader?

4. Create a list of the language used by and to describe each **character**. Add notes as to what the language suggests about each of them. Focus particularly on Monsieur and Madame Loisel.

5. See if you can think of two exam questions that might come up about this text, and then see if you can answer them! Here is an example of the kind of question you might write: 'How does the author characterise Monsieur and Madame Loisel? You must refer to the author's use of language as well as the character's actions.'

6. How do you feel about Madame Loisel? Use evidence to support your answer.

A Hero (pages 84–90 in the student book)

- R.K. Narayan (1906–2001) was born and lived in India but wrote all of his work in English.

- He is one of the most influential of India's writers, and is credited with helping to bring Indian literature to the rest of the world.

- He set his stories in the fictional town of Malgudi and his stories are generally about the people's lives and interactions.

Meaning: What is the text about?

Have a look over this text again. What is the author telling us about? Is it just Swami's story or is there a deeper message?

Here are some notes on the language and structure of the text.

Language

- The description of the mother 'rocking the cradle' in line 32 reinforces the idea that she is treating Swami like a baby.

- Hyperbole is used by Swami's father in lines 11–14 to reinforce his point that courage can help you achieve anything.

Structure

- The **ellipsis** in line 93 could represent Swami holding his breath.

- The short sentences in lines 101–102 are used to build tension, as the reader waits to see what Swami has seen.

Some activities to help you revise the text

1. Look at the notes on the text above and try to add to them, thinking about the linguistic and structural devices used by the author and the effects they create.

2. How is Swami's father portrayed in the story? Give examples of the language used to describe him and comment on how they have an effect on the reader.

3. Explain how the sentence structure of lines 69–78 reflects Swami's state of mind.

4. Who is the hero in the title of the story and why? At different times, we see it could be different characters.

5. What is the impact of the last line of the story? What could be the implicit meaning of the phrase 'giving him up'?

6. Two students were set the following question. Have a look at their responses – which do you think is the best and why?

At times in this piece we see vivid images from Swami's imagination. How effective is this in helping us to sympathise with Swami as a character?

Student A

I don't think that Swami is very sympathetic as a character. He comes over as a scared little boy and seems silly. All of his fantasies only make him seem ridiculous as his family is only through the other side of the wall. His father seems like a tyrant and the women of the story are presented as weak.

Student B

The passages that relate Swami's imagination of what could happen to him help us to understand him better. He has been told stories of devils and demons which terrify him. The image of 'Munisami's father, who spat out blood...' would be horrifying for a child of his age and his idea that the devil will 'pull him out and tear him' shows us just how scared he must be.

Notes

King Schahriar and His Brother (from *The Arabian Nights*) (pages 91–96 in the student book)

- This story dates from over a thousand years ago and is the first story from a collection called *The Arabian Nights* (also known as *The One Thousand and One Nights*).

- It has been translated from the original Arabic. All the stories come from ancient Arabia – the area we now call the Middle East – or from India or China.

- This story is the first in the sequence and is the **setting** for all the rest of the stories, as Scheherazade becomes the narrator for all the stories that follow.

Scheherazade seized by the King – an illustration from The Arabian Nights, *1895.*

Meaning: What is the text about?

Read the text once again. Try to think about the meaning of the text beyond the simple storyline – what is the point of the story?

Here are some notes on the language and structure of the text.

Language

- The way in which Scheherazade is described sets her up as a reliable narrator for the stories that follow: 'Her father had given her the best masters in philosophy, medicine, history and the fine arts, and besides all this, her beauty excelled that of any girl in the kingdom of Persia.'

- The **tone** changes in the third paragraph as the Sultan discovers his wife's deception. The language changes from him surrounding his wife with the 'finest dresses' and 'most beautiful jewels' to stark descriptions of how he slaughtered a fresh wife every day.

Structure

- The long sentence at the beginning of the text highlights the length of the dynasty's reign and the great expanse of its kingdom.

Some activities to help you revise the text

1. Look at the notes on the text above and try to add to them, thinking about the linguistic and structural devices used by the author and the effects they create.

2. The phrasing in the story is very sparse and gives us very little description. Highlight phrases that create a picture of Scheherazade and that give you an insight into her character. Add in comments on what effect these are intended to have on the audience.

3. What is the impact of the use of **superlatives** throughout the piece? See if you can highlight all of them.

4. How are siblings represented in the story? See if you can find some examples of the language used to describe the relationships between siblings.

5. While Scheherazade is clearly the protagonist, Sultan Schahriar is also a key character. How is he portrayed?

Chapter 3: Unprepared Non-fiction

In this section of the revision guide we will look at the skills you need for the unprepared non-fiction section of your exam.

- This is Section A of Paper 1.
- The questions on this part of the paper are worth 20 marks in total.
- You should spend 45 minutes on this part of the exam.
- The text will be non-fiction but could be any type of writing, from a newspaper article or travelogue to an autobiography or leaflet. It will be of a similar type to the writing included in the Section A anthology texts.
- After some short questions totalling 8 marks, there will be one long-answer question worth 12 marks, which you should treat as an essay. You will be expected to analyse and comment on specific examples and quotations.

What you will learn in this chapter

- active reading skills such as **skimming** and **scanning**
- how to prepare for short-answer questions
- planning skills
- how you will be marked in the exam.

What does the examiner want?

For this part of the exam you will be expected to demonstrate your skills in assessment objective 2: Reading. By now you should be familiar with what that means. Have a look at the assessment objectives and see if you can put them into your own words.

AO2 (i): Read and understand texts with insight and engagement.

AO2 (ii): Develop and sustain interpretations of writers' ideas and perspectives.

AO2 (iii): Understand and make some evaluation of how the writers use linguistic and structural devices to achieve their effects.

Active reading skills

In exams you need to make the most of your time. There is no point in simply reading the unprepared passage through without actively engaging with it. A good way to approach a text is:

Skim $\longrightarrow$ Scan $\longrightarrow$ Intensive reading

- Skimming: Casting your eye over the piece to get the gist of what it is about.
- Scanning: Looking for particular information, such as what the text will cover and names, places and key facts.
- Intensive reading: Accurate reading for detail and techniques, thinking about what you are being asked to comment on. Focus on these aspects as you complete this close reading.

What should you be looking for in your active reading?

When you are looking at your unprepared passage, you need to think about the three vital elements:

- *Purpose:* Why has the text been written? What type of writing is it?
- *Audience:* Who has the text been written for and how do you know that?
- *Technique:* What kinds of techniques has the writer used to make their point?

A student was asked to practise these skills when reading the text below. There are boxes for how the student annotated the text differently each time they read it. See if you can fill in the gaps provided in these boxes, particularly those looking at purpose, audience and technique.

Audience

____

____

____

Skim

The piece is about ______

____

Looking for support and updating supporters on ________________

____

____

Scan

____

____

____

____

____

____

____

____

____

Malaria Mission

Day 43 – Update

Sarah and I have now been here at the orphanage for 40 days and it has become a real home for us. It is a place of fun, laughter and joy. We have seen a huge improvement in the health and well being of the children here – which really is down to your support! Ejemhen, who you might remember from my previous posts, has been recovering well from the malarial bout that she was suffering due to the medicines and goods that our supporters have provided, and her brother Dollar seems to be in the clear with no diagnosis of malaria. We are sure this is down to the mosquito nets that have been provided to us. Having us here with our medical background is helping too.

How to give your support!

All you need to do to support us is to send your donations of food, toys, medicines or mosquito nets to the address on our contact us page and it will all come directly to the orphanage, here in Nigeria. Do donate money too, as this will help us to be able to stay here and carry out our work. Please, please don't stop giving as this is the only way we can continue to make a real difference here.

Active reading

'!' shows ______________

Hyperbole has the effect of ________________

____

'your'________________

____

makes the story personal.

Sub-headings____________

____

'All you need to do' is informal and ____________

____

Use of the **imperative**____

____

Colloquialism: ____________

____

What's next?

Now that we feel we have really found our feet here we are ready to start to pass on some knowledge, to share what we have learnt and to establish some good practices here in the orphanage. We are hoping to be able to start training some of the staff here on how to deliver the anti-malarial medicines you have provided – watch this space!

Emily

Audience

_____

_____

_____

_____

Purpose

_____

_____

_____

Exam-Style Questions

Answer the following questions about the text:

1. Who are the two children mentioned in the extract? (2 marks)

2. Look again at the 'Day 43 – Update' section of the text. Give three words or phrases that the author uses to establish how happy she is at the orphanage. (3 marks)

3. Describe in your own words what the doctors are trying to achieve at the orphanage. (3 marks)

4. How does the writer try to persuade us to donate to the mission? In your answer you should write about:

   - the writer's thoughts and feelings
   - the story of Ejemhen and Dollar
   - particular words, phrases and techniques.

   You may include brief quotations from the passage to support your answer. (12 marks)

Use your time wisely!

Look again at the questions above – you need to consider how long you would spend on each question. You have 45 minutes for this section of the paper. In that time you need to:

- skim
- scan
- intensively read
- answer the short-answer questions
- plan for the long-answer question
- write your long answer
- read over what you have written.

This means that you need to divide your time up wisely. Look at the Top Tip box for some tips for how to work through your question paper.

TOP TIP ✓

- Look at what the question asks you to do. If you only have to give information then do just that – don't waste time explaining or rephrasing.

- Be sure to put things into your own words when you are asked to do so.

- Don't spend more than a couple of minutes on a one-, two- or three-mark question.

- Take your time on the 12-mark close analysis question (the last in the section).

The long answer

Let's spend some time looking at the longer question in this part of the exam. This question will be worth 12 marks so it is worth getting it right. First of all, have a look at the extract below and practise your skimming and scanning skills.

The Bush Border Bus to South Africa

Paul Theroux is a world-renowned travel writer who lived for many years in Malawi. In later life he challenged himself to travel from Cairo to Cape Town overland and this is an excerpt from his book *Dark Star Safari*, which chronicled that journey. In the extract he is preparing to leave Zimbabwe.

sentry: usually a soldier stationed to keep guard
raptor: a bird of prey

bush bus: a minibus used in the African countryside
bougainvillea: a beautiful tropical plant

porkpie hat: a small hat made of felt or straw

circumscribed: restricted or confined

pious: showing religious devotion
Goad: God
jinny: journey
His Divine Hayns: His Divine Hands

Southward one hot morning down the hot straight road out of Harare, a farm fence on either side, past the grazing land of white-owned cattle ranches with names like 'Broad Acres' and 'Sunset', a sentry* at every gate, a raptor* on most telephone poles, always a watching hawk here: to South Africa. What a pleasure it was to leave Harare on a sunny day, sitting in an upholstered seat in this long-distance bush bus*, on the road that began in Cairo.

Low white farm buildings were dwarfed by bougainvillea* as high as apple trees. Little rivulets and streams, the land so flat and rural I might have been on a back road in Ohio. But every now and then there was an emphatic reminder of Africa: a bungalow-sized anthill, an African in a blue suit and porkpie hat* pedaling a bike, a fat-bellied zebra and a skinny horse grazing side by side, an ostrich under a tree, a monkey picking his teeth on a fencepost and the distinct signs of farm invasions – crude huts, the Zimbabwe flag, stacks of gum tree poles for another hut, and in large farm fields small circumscribed* maize patches where there should have been a whole hillside of stalks. In the bright dusty town of Dryton twenty-two cars were lined up at the gas station because of the shortage of fuel.

The pious* voice of the driver animated the bus's loudspeaker: 'With the help of Almighty Goad* we will be guided on our jinny* and shall be safe in His Divine Hanyns*.'

Had I chuckled? Perhaps. All I ever thought of when on an African bus was the standing headline, 'Many Dead in Bus Plunge Horror.'

Answering the question

So, you have used your active reading skills to get all you can from the passage. You should now be able to pick out the following:

- *Purpose*: Why has the text been written? What type of writing is it?

- *Audience*: Who has the text been written for and how do you know that?

- *Technique*: What kinds of techniques has the writer used to make his point?

These aren't the questions you will be asked, but having a clear knowledge of them will help you in the longer question you will face. That question might be something like this:

How would you go about answering this? The first thing to do is to make sure you understand the question. One student was asked to put it into their own words and they rephrased it like this:

How does the writer give us a picture of the Zimbabwe he sees? Think about the things he describes, whether he enjoys the journey and why and then look at the language and structural devices he uses to communicate the story to us.

TOP TIP ✔

Sometimes if you are stuck with a question, putting it into your own words can help you get unstuck! You don't need to write it down!

Planning

It is a good idea to write a plan for your 12-mark question so that you know what to write about and when to write it. It will help you to focus on the question and ensure you are including the right aspects. Have a go at writing your own plan for this answer.

Writing your answer

Now that you have your plan, write your answer to the question. Remember that in this section of the paper you will be marked on what you say (your interpretation of the text), not how you say it (your writing skills).

Checking it over

The final stage in a long answer like this is to check over the work you have done. There are several ways to do this, but following is a list of suggestions:

- Start by looking back at your plan and cross out the things you have included – if you don't use the plan there is no point in writing it.
- Read over the answer as though you are reading it aloud inside your head.
- Try to see it with fresh eyes – what have you missed?
- Take one last look at the question and make sure you have answered it – there are numerous students who lose marks in the exam because they haven't answered the question that is printed on the exam paper.

How the question is marked

Below is an example of one candidate's answer to the question you have been working on.

> The impression that the writer creates of Zimbabwe is quite complex. At first he describes it as being similar to his homeland of Ohio – 'flat and rural' – but then we start to see the aspects that are 'emphatic reminders of Africa'. He paints a picture of a rural lifestyle where people in suits are riding around on bicycles, where game animals are grazing with livestock, ostriches and monkeys. This makes it seem very foreign to a Western reader. He uses a metaphor for the 'bungalow-sized anthills' to exaggerate the image of nature being as powerful as the human community.
>
> He also shows us images of unrest whereby he describes the scenes of farm invasion and fuel shortages – it is not a simple place or a 'perfect Africa'. He uses imagery in the first paragraph to give the feeling of being watched as he likens sentries at the farm gates to 'a watching hawk'.
>
> Despite this he seems to be happy. He describes his journey as 'a pleasure' and seems comfortable in his 'upholstered seat'.
>
> In his final paragraph he invites the reader to be a part of the picture he has painted by using a rhetorical question 'Had I chuckled?' making us an implicit part of the journey and taking us with him to the African scene.

How did the student do? Did he/she fulfil the brief? Let's look back at the assessment objectives for the paper:

AO 2 (i): Read and understand texts with insight and engagement.	Has the student understood what the text is about and used quotations to support what they say about it? Yes!
AO 2 (ii): Develop and sustain interpretations of writers' ideas and perspectives.	Has the student given their own impression of the author's experiences, feelings and views? Yes!
AO 2 (iii): Understand and make some evaluation of how the writers use linguistic and structural devices to achieve their effects.	Has the student said how effective the writer has been in using language and structural techniques to convey an image of Zimbabwe? Yes!

Examiners are also given an assessment grid to use when they mark work. It looks like this:

Level	Mark	Criteria
Level 0	0	• Candidate hasn't written anything!
Level 1	1–3	• Candidate understands the text and has selected some quotations but these are not wholly relevant. • Candidate doesn't make much reference to linguistic or structural devices. • Candidate doesn't really connect the use of these devices to the way a writer presents ideas or **themes**.

Level	Mark	Criteria
Level 2	4–6	• Candidate has a good understanding of the text and some of the references the candidate makes to the text are in line with the candidate's ideas. • Candidate has some ideas about how language, structure and form are used by the writer. • Candidate is starting to link these ideas to the impact they have on the reader.
Level 3	7–9	• Candidate shows a thorough understanding of the text and the candidate's references to it are relevant. • Candidate understands how the writer has used language, structure and form for effect. • Candidate can explain how these techniques are used to create effects.
Level 4	10–12	• Candidate has a very good understanding of the text and can refer to it in a way which is wholly relevant. • Candidate has a very thorough understanding of language, structure and form and how these are used to create effects. • Candidate's interpretations of how writers use these devices to present their ideas and themes is sustained and well developed.

Which level do you think the exam marker would have chosen for this answer? Why? Here is what the exam marker said about the student's answer:

Examiner's comments

This response is well focused on the question in hand and remains focused throughout. It is a detailed response which makes good use of references to the text, demonstrating a good knowledge of technical language, and clear evidence that the student has engaged well with the excerpt. Excellent skills of analysis and interpretation are shown throughout. This answer is somewhat on the short side and there may have been some points which could have been explored further, or expanded upon, but the level of technical analysis is excellent and in reality there is not enough time to comment on all the aspects of the extract.

Marks = 12

Have a go at marking your own work using this grid as well as the assessment objectives.

Examiners:

- look for what you *have* done, not what you *haven't* done
- are expected to mark positively
- will give as many marks as they can for an answer – they will not withhold marks just because they don't want to give out full marks
- can mark crossed-out work if there seems to be nothing there to replace it
- can be affected by sloppy handwriting: If your work is illegible, they will find it hard to mark it.

Chapter 4: Writing in a Wide Range of Forms and Genres

In this chapter of the book we will focus on the skills you will need for the writing aspects of your International GCSE or Certificate in English Language. We will look at the different types of writing you will have to produce, how that writing will be marked and what skills you will require for each type of writing.

What you will learn in this chapter

- how to plan and structure your writing
- the different types of writing you will have to produce
- what skills you will require for each type of writing
- how the writing will be marked.

The writing triplets

All the writing tasks that you will undertake have been split into the following three writing triplets:

- writing to explore, imagine, entertain
- writing to inform, explain, describe
- writing to argue, persuade, advise.

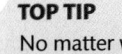

TOP TIP

No matter which triplet you are using, you always need to consider three vital elements:

- purpose
- audience
- technique.

Writing required for International GCSE Specification A

There are two different 'routes' through Specification A but both will require some writing.

Route 1	Route 2
Paper 1: Section B (10 marks)	**Paper 1: Section B** (10 marks)
Writing triplet not specified	Writing triplet not specified
Paper 1: Section C (20 marks)	**Paper 1: Section C** (20 marks)
Inform, explain, describe	Inform, explain, describe
Paper 2: Section 2 (15 marks)	**Paper 3: Writing Section** (40 marks)
Explore, imagine, entertain	Explore, imagine, entertain
or	*or*
Argue, persuade, advise	Argue, persuade, advise

Writing required for the Edexcel Certificate in English Language

If you are studying for the Edexcel Certificate in English Language, the route is as follows:

Paper 1: Section B (10 marks)
Writing triplet not specified
Paper 1: Section C (20 marks)
Inform, explain, describe
Paper 2: Section 2 (24 marks)
Explore, imagine, entertain
and
Argue, persuade, advise

What the examiner wants

The following are the assessment objectives for the writing elements. On the left are the assessment objectives and on the right are explanations of what the assessment objectives mean.

AO3 (i): Communicate clearly and appropriately, using and adapting forms for different readers and purposes.	Writing that is easy to understand and that skilfully uses the right *techniques* for its *purpose and audience*.
AO3 (ii): Organise ideas into sentences, paragraphs and whole texts using a variety of linguistic and structural features.	Writing that is *'shaped'* correctly, using *sentences and paragraphs* as well as *ordering*, and that uses the right *techniques for the purpose*.
AO3 (iii): Use a range of sentence structures effectively, with accurate punctuation and spelling.	*Grammar* is correct on a *word*, *punctuation and sentence* level and *sentences* are chosen to *create an effect*.

> Above all, the examiner wants to see writing that is consciously crafted. This means that it has been thoughtfully organised, shaped and sculpted into something that is effective and pleasurable to read.

Perfect planning

Why do we plan?

A plan:

- will help you to write faster and more confidently
- will give a strong beginning, middle and end to your piece of writing
- can remind you of the techniques you want to use
- can organise your ideas into a logical and clear order.

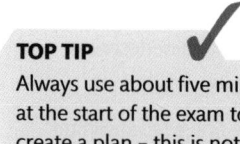

TOP TIP
Always use about five minutes at the start of the exam to create a plan – this is not time wasted as it will mean you use the rest of your time in a more effective way.

Methods of planning

◊ Have a look at the three plans on the following page. Which do you think is the most effective and why?

Plan A

Mobile phones can help you search the web.

Can be disruptive.

Write to argue

Pupils more engaged if allowed phones in class.

Technology important.

Plan B

Write to argue: Should mobile phones be allowed in classrooms?

Intro:
- rise of technology
- importance of mobile phones
- youth culture and mobile phones.

Paragraph 1: Mobiles as a learning tool
- useful for searching the web
- posting blogs about studies
- sharing ideas within the classroom.

Paragraph 2: Different subjects
- mobiles in Media Studies – making films
- mobiles in PE – sharing good techniques
- mobiles in English – recording speaking and listening.

Paragraph 3: Drawbacks
- phones disrupting lessons
- students posting about teachers
- reliance on technology.

Plan C

Mobile phones
- useful for searching the web
- importance of mobile phones
- rise of technology
- youth culture and mobile phones
- sharing ideas within the classroom
- students posting about teachers
- posting blogs about studies
- mobiles in Media Studies – making films
- mobiles in PE – sharing good techniques
- reliance on technology
- mobiles in English – recording speaking and listening
- phones disrupting lessons.

These methods of planning would work equally well if they all contained the same level of information, but Plan B will allow the student to present a very clear and logical piece of writing.

Perfect planning

Use any shape of plan you prefer – either a spider diagram or a bullet-pointed list.

Jot down all your ideas to begin with so that you don't forget anything.

Next think about how you will organise them and which ideas go together.

Organise your ideas into paragraphs. You could number them to make this process as quick as possible. You might have already put your ideas into paragraphs as you're going along, like the student who created plan B.

Some students find it helpful to include in their plan a list of the techniques they want to use in their writing. This can help you to remember to use the correct techniques for the purpose. For example, you might make a list like this:

- sentence structures for effect
- rhetorical question
- triplet/rule of three
- alliteration
- **formal** language.

Make your own list of the techniques you feel confident with. You can use this list as a starting point.

How to organise your writing

There are several factors involved in organising a piece of text:

- order of points
- paragraphing
- connectives
- sentences
- punctuation.

◊ Have a look at the candidate's work below and see if you can offer advice on how to improve the organisation. Two comments have been added for you as examples.

Some people argue that mobile phones should not be allowed in schools, but the debate rages on as there are those who feel that the benefits of phones in the classrooms outweigh the disadvantages. It can be a very helpful tool for learning as students can use them in a range of subjects. In PE they can be used to record short clips of good examples of techniques – these can then be shared with the students of the class so that they can see what they should aspire to. One great disadvantage though is that students can use their phones to make malicious posts on social networking sites either about pupils or about teachers which would cause great upset and would be an impediment to learning and to the social harmony of the school. They could also be used in subjects like English and Media Studies where they could be used for making films or recordings of students' work for submission as coursework. Are we however, becoming too reliant on technology in this generation? Some would argue that it is important for us to be able to use other methods of learning and that as this younger generation spends so much time outside of school engaging with technology they ought to spend their school hours without it. It could also be helpful in schools where there is limited access to computers as students could use their smartphones to search the web and to produce research without even having to leave the classroom which would no doubt make some subjects a lot simpler.

Example comments

> *Paragraphs: You can see just by glancing at the text that there are no paragraphs, which will make it difficult for the reader to follow the* **argument**.

> *Punctuation: There are one or two examples of good punctuation but perhaps some more interesting forms may have been added for effect.*

Sentence structures and punctuation

◊ Can you remember assessment objective 3 (iii)? See if you can fill in the gaps, choosing from the word bank:

Word bank

AO3 (iii): Use a _____ of sentence structures _____, with _____ punctuation and spelling.	range properly exciting number well effectively selection nice accurate

It is important that you understand the different sentence structures and types of punctuation that are available to you and the effect that they can have on a reader.

Sentence structures

It is a good idea to know about the different sentence types so that you are confident with using them. Here is what you need to know:

- A main clause generally contains a subject, a verb and an object, e.g. 'Susan (subject) likes (verb) tea (object)'.

- A subordinate clause is a clause that adds information to a main clause but that cannot stand alone as a sentence. It usually starts with a subordinating conjunction or a relative pronoun and contains a subject and a verb. An example might be 'when (subordinating conjunction) it contains (verb) milk and sugar (subject)'.

So what kinds of sentences can we build with these clauses?

Sentence type	Structure	Effect
Simple	One single clause.	Gives basic information or makes a bold statement.
Compound	More than one main clause, bound together using punctuation or a connective.	Allows the writer to connect two ideas or pieces of information together.
Complex	More than one clause, where one is a subordinate clause.	Allows the author to mention information that is descriptive or less important.

◊ Read the following three sentences. Which is simple, which is compound and which is complex?

It was a sunny day. Saj woke up feeling very happy and he leapt out of bed. While he was getting dressed, he noticed that the contents of his school bag had fallen all over the floor.

Let's think again about the three vital elements:

- *Purpose*: Sentence structures can be used to shape your writing to the appropriate style – complex sentences might be more appropriate for descriptive writing, while simple sentences can be useful in informative writing.

- *Audience*: You can have a great effect on your audience by selecting your sentence styles carefully – a short sentence can have a real impact.

- *Technique*: Varying your sentence structures can make your writing richer and more enjoyable.

Punctuation

◊ The following table of punctuation has been mixed up. Ensure you know the different types of punctuation by linking each type to its name and effect on the reader.

Punctuation	Name	Effect
.	Speech marks	Creates a pause in a sentence or shows a change in a clause.
,	Pair of dashes	Shows a pause in thought, missing text or a pause for tension.
– ... –	Comma	Shows the reader where a sentence ends.
...	Full stop	Used to enclose direct speech to show that a character or person is speaking.
'...'	Ellipsis	Allows the writer to add in a subordinate clause.

Writing to explore, imagine, entertain

- *Writing to explore*: Writing that investigates or closely examines your thoughts and feelings on a certain topic.

- *Writing to imagine*: Writing that tells a story or creates a scene.

- *Writing to entertain*: Writing that powerfully captivates readers and gives them enjoyment.

Activities to help your revision

1. Write about a childhood memory, exploring your thoughts and feelings about it.

2. Write about a place you have visited, exploring how you felt about it.

3. Imagine you are very old and you are looking back over your lifetime. Describe your most important memories.

4. Write a story that begins with the words 'As I looked closer, it seemed as if the city was disappearing'.

◊ Have a go at planning one or more of these questions (see pages 66–68 for advice on perfect planning). Use any format you like – a spider diagram, a bullet-point list or a structure of your own choosing – but make sure it is thorough enough to guide you through writing the piece.

◊ Why not also have a go at writing answers to one or more of the questions? If you are studying for the International GCSE, you should allow yourself about 45 minutes of planning and writing time. Certificate students will only have about 22 minutes for each of the two questions they have to complete. See what you can produce under timed conditions.

TOP TIP ✓
Notice that the first two questions provoke you to explore while the second two expect you to imagine. It is unlikely you will face an 'entertain' question, but you are expected to write in an entertaining fashion for every question.

Entertaining your reader

There are three ways to entertain your reader:

- Engage your reader straight away.

- Keep your reader interested.

- Provide an effective ending.

Engaging your reader: How to begin your writing

Look at the three opening sentences below and think about which is the most effective and why:

- It was a warm sunny day when Jenny and Louise set off for their picnic.

- Stutter. Slurp. Creak.

- A freezing wind whipped about my face as I looked up at the bleak hospital building. The November sleet stung my face and I knew I had to go inside.

> Gives an idea of character and setting but isn't very imaginative.
>
> Interesting and different but doesn't give the reader a sense of what kind of story this will be.
>
> Establishes a sense of character, place and emotion as well as a hint of the story to follow.

Let's consider the three vital elements:

- *Purpose*: A good opening should make it clear what kind of narrative awaits, as well as establishing the style of writing.

- *Audience*: Your audience wants to be able to identify with your characters from the start through a sense of their situation and feelings.

- *Technique*: Your writing should be shaped using interesting techniques in order to hook your readers' attention. We'll consider that more in the next section.

Keep the reader interested

◊ Compare the two pieces of writing below. Which do you think is more likely to engage the reader and why?

A

Jenny and Mike were walking when they heard a rustling sound behind them. They looked round but didn't see anything so they just kept walking. It was a sunny day but a bit windy. They thought they heard the noise again as they walked further on.

B

We held hands as we walked on that beautiful, blue-sky day, the wind gently tugging at my hair and playing through the leaves of the trees. Mike looked over and smiled at me, a look I'll never forget now. It was then that we first heard the noise. It was as if there was a creature in the long grass, moving stealthily towards us. I told myself I was being silly, and walked on.

◊ Now look at the examiner's feedback below and see if you can match each one to either extract A or B.

> The story seems a bit obvious. It is not very interesting and there is little sense of the two characters who are introduced. The order of the story seems a bit odd.

> The story is starting to develop well as the reader learns about the relationship between the characters. The reader gets a sense of foreboding – that something terrible is about to happen.

> Interesting word choices and phrasing as well as some sophisticated language techniques such as alliteration and personification help to enrich the text. Sentences are used to build the tension.

> Word choices and phrasing are somewhat *clichéd* and there is very little description in the story. Sentences tend to be long and rambling without any effect – the focus is too much on narrative and not enough on style.

Language techniques

This is a selection of some of the language techniques that an examiner might want to see in your work – these help you to enrich your writing.

Technique	Description	Example
Alliteration	Repetition of a syllable sound in several words near each other in a phrase.	'the silent stillness'
Assonance	Repetition of a vowel sound in several words near each other in a phrase.	'glossy clot'
Hyperbole	Exaggeration for effect.	'it is the most frightening thing you will ever see'
Metaphor	A comparison of two objects that implies that one is the same as the other.	'a blanket of fog'
Onomatopoeia	A word that resembles the sound that it describes.	'trickle' or 'snap'
Personification	Application of human characteristics to an inanimate object.	'the car roared and snarled'
Simile	A comparison of two things that suggests that one is like another.	'as fast as wild horses'

◊ How many of these can you spot in extract B above?

TOP TIP ✔

Some students write a list of the techniques they feel confident of in the corner of their exam paper when they are in the planning stage and then check that they have included at least one of each when they read their work over.

Effective endings

The two most important sentences you will write are the first and the last as they set and seal the tone. Your ending should:

- create an impact on the reader
- answer the question, or in some way 'sum up' the story you are telling
- show your flair in writing.

Again, let's consider those three vital elements:

- *Purpose*: A good final paragraph should complete the narrative while still being true to the style.
- *Audience*: The ending of your story should make your work stand out in the mind of the reader and provide a satisfying finish.
- *Technique*: This is your last chance to make an impact on the reader so do try to use the same standard of writing you have employed throughout your piece.

Crafting your writing

The best pieces of writing are usually ones that the writer has prepared with much thought and care, shaping what he/she says. This can be difficult under exam conditions, but good planning, a wide knowledge of the appropriate techniques and careful revision will help to give you the time to craft your work carefully. Have a look at the excerpt below and think about ways you could improve it. An example has been included to help get you started.

You could add a simile by changing 'pointy' to 'hawk-like'.

The car pulled up alongside the alleyway and Will crouched lower into the shadows. The man's pointy nose could be seen through the window of the car, even at this time of night. Will thought he could stay and hide or run away.

Writing to inform, explain, describe

- *Writing to inform*: Writing that conveys information to readers so that they are in command of the facts of a process or topic.
- *Writing to explain*: Writing that explains how or why something is as it is.
- *Writing to describe*: Writing that conjures a picture of a situation or process for the reader.

Activities to help your revision

1. Write about a time when you were scared.

2. The mayor of your town would like to know more about your school and you have been selected to write to her or him with more information. Write to inform the mayor about your school and what happens there on an ordinary day.

3. How is climate change affecting our world?

4. Write about your most interesting holiday experience.

◊ Can you work out which of these questions expect you to *inform*, which are *explain* questions and which ones ask you to *describe*?

◊ Now you have a go – choose one of these questions and write a practice response. This should take you around 50 minutes.

Conventions of the writing styles

Writing style	Convention	Explanation
All	Writing is organised into paragraphs.	In order to discuss a process or topic in depth, paragraphs allow the reader to follow the steps or sub-topics involved.
All	Connectives link paragraphs.	This allows the reader to anticipate what is coming next.
All	Ideas are carefully thought through and organised.	The writer must think about what the audience wants to learn and plan how and when to present the information.
Inform	Statistics are used.	Numbers and figures can give your reader a clearer picture of the topic.
Explain	Writing is in the present tense.	This gives the reader a sense of the contemporary nature of the topic.
Describe	Writing can become personal.	In this form of writing the reader wants to learn about the narrator.

◊ Next look at the following table and think about which styles of writing the conventions and explanations refer to. See if you can complete the table.

Style of writing	Convention	Explanation
	May use the imperative mood, or command language.	Gives a clearer idea on the topic.
	May use a formal style but also use pronouns such as 'we', 'our' or 'I'.	Allows writers to impart information about a subject that they are involved with.
	Refers to the senses to enrich the narrative.	Conveys to the reader a fuller picture of the story.

Writing to argue, persuade, advise

- *Writing to argue*: Writing that links a number of ideas to prove or justify a viewpoint.

- *Writing to persuade*: Writing that is designed to influence readers' opinions so that they agree with the writer.

- *Writing to advise*: Writing that proposes a course of action to the reader, offering suggestions or ideas.

Activities to help your revision

1. Some sports scientists have proposed that one hour of sport should be introduced into the daily timetable of all students at secondary school. Give your views on this topic, arguing either in favour of compulsory sport in school or against it.

2. Write a letter persuading your local council to start a new youth project in your area.

3. Write an article for your school magazine that gives younger students exam advice.

4. Write a letter to your head teacher persuading her or him to give all students some free time in their timetable.

◊ Try writing a sample plan for one of these exam questions – think about how you will structure your work and what you might want to include. There is more information on planning in the next section.

Remember – if you are a Certificate student or a Route 1 International GCSE student you will face this kind of question in the exam. However, Route 2 students will already have covered this in their coursework.

If you are a Certificate student you should only spend about 22 minutes on this question in the exam (and in your practice!). Route 1 students will have about 45 minutes.

Writing to argue

When writing to argue, you will be expected to:

- present a clear, logical argument
- show both sides of an argument
- offer your **opinion**
- use evidence in support of your argument
- structure your argument using paragraphs
- use a formal tone
- express yourself with clarity.

◊ Look at the work below and see if you can fill in the examiner's comments using the phrases provided in the word bank:

Sport in school has become less and less important over the years. Children in this country are becoming obese and something needs to be done. Some scientists think it would be a good idea to put more sport in schools but I am not sure, not everyone likes sport so it might make people unhappy.

One reason to have more sport is so that people will get fitter. If they do more running around and exercising the students will be more likely not to be unhealthy and then will have a better lifestyle. I have heard that if you are healthy you might also get better grades.

One reason not to have more sport is that people will be unhappy. I, for one, don't like PE and think I would be unhappy to have to do more. It is boring and I am not good at it so I think it should not happen.

Examiner's comments

While the writing does communicate a _____ _____, the register is too _____, often relying on personal feelings. While there is some use of _____, there is little evidence that the text has been logically organised within those paragraphs as ideas are confused in places. The _____ is inappropriate and, while some attempt has been used to make _____ between the paragraphs, the linking phrases are repetitive and mundane.

Word bank

paragraphs to organise ideas

word choice

connections

informal

broadly appropriate argument

Writing to persuade

When writing to persuade, you will be expected to:

- choose a style that is appropriate to your audience
- stress one side of an argument
- use rhetoric to influence your reader
- use **anecdotes**, statistics and evidence to support your opinion
- express yourself with clarity.

What is rhetoric?

Rhetoric is language that is purposefully designed to persuade or impress a reader. It is primarily considered to be a skill in speaking but there are many techniques that we can use in written persuasion as well.

Following are just a few rhetorical devices you might want to use.

Rhetorical device	Example	Effect on the reader
Triplet/rule of three	Smoking is unhealthy for your body, your bank balance and your social life.	A list of three reinforces your argument.
Hyperbole	The current state of school meals is criminal.	Exaggerating a situation provokes an emotional response in the reader – in this case, horror or shock.
Rhetorical question	Would you want to live like this?	An unanswered question is thought-provoking and can encourage readers to agree with the author.
Personal pronoun	I know that you agree with me on this.	Using 'I', 'we' and 'you' makes readers feel that the argument is personal and that they have to engage with it.
Repetition	Obesity is dangerous. Packaged foods are dangerous. Food marketing is dangerous.	The key word from your argument is the one that will remain in your reader's mind.

Writing to advise

When writing to advise, you will be expected to:

- reassure your audience that you are an authority on the topic

- offer your opinion

- use evidence so that people know you are an authority on the topic

- structure your idea using paragraphs

- use the right tone for your audience (if you are writing for teenagers, you can adapt your language to some extent, while still remembering that your key audience is the examiner; the examiner wants to see writing that is standardised and grammatically correct)

- make it memorable.

◊ Have a look at the exam paper below – which examiner's response do you think is the one that matches it?

Exam question

Imagine that you are giving advice to new students who will be joining your school in September – what are the best pieces of advice that you can give them about their new school?

Answer

One must always be on time for classes. Do not be shy about asking the way – your peers and colleagues are here for you in order to help you to survive the gauntlet of your first few weeks and none of us want to see you come in for any undue punishments due to a lack of geographical knowledge. Also, do try to show the teachers that you are a willing pupil and you are here to learn, it is good to have them on side. While the student body of this institution is not a judgmental one, you may want to think about your uniform for the first day – we like our ties short and our shirts untucked. That way one will become a part of the crowd.

Examiner A's response

This work shows clear evidence of planning as it covers a lot of points and makes these well. It offers sound advice and is a useful document. The vocabulary is excellent and sentences are well structured.

Examiner B's response

The tone of this writing is not appropriate for the audience as it is too formal, and while it presents a lot of advice, this is not structured particularly well and jumps from one point to another. There is no evidence of paragraphing.

Chapter 5: Preparing for the Exam

You will know well in advance when your exam is and you can never start preparing for it too early. Here are some of the things you can do to prepare for your exam:

- **Check your coursework!** If you are taking International GCSE Specification A and you are following Route 2, you will have to submit coursework so make sure you check it through carefully (Route 1 and Certificate students do not have to do coursework). Remember that your coursework marks and your exam marks are added together to give a final grade. So, before you think about the exam, make sure your coursework is up to scratch and that it is all complete.

- **Make a revision timetable.** Look over the sections of the exam paper that you need to prepare for and think about how and when you will revise for them. Think about when you will do your best revision (probably not late at night or when you are distracted!) and make sure you have that time set aside.

- **Clear a space.** It is good to have somewhere you can work quietly, without clutter or confusion around you.

- **Work through your revision guide.** You need to cover all the sections of the guide to know you are prepared, but you don't have to do it in order. Start with whichever section you want.

- **Make your own revision notes.** Writing things out will help you to remember them. Print off clean copies of the poems, prose and non-fiction texts and annotate them yourself. You could then stick them up where you are revising.

- **Use a variety of revision strategies.** Examples include: Colour-coding your notes, writing sticky notes, revising online, using mnemonics to remember key terminology, and completing revision questions and practice papers.

As English is not only a content-based subject but also a skills-based subject, you do need to make sure you allow plenty of time for your revision. However, here are some things you could do in the days immediately before the exam:

- **Re-read the anthology texts.** Read them over and annotate them for *purpose*, *audience* and *techniques*.

- **Exam practice questions.** Use the exam practice questions in this book and in the e-book to practise your skills.

- **Timed conditions.** Make sure any practice you do, whether it is for the anthology section, the unprepared non-fiction or the writing part of the exam, is under timed conditions. There is no point in taking too much time as you will have limited time in the exam.

- **Check you have everything ready!** You will need black ink pens (take a few for reassurance) for the exam so make sure you have some ready.

What to expect in the exam

If you are using this revision guide you could be studying for the International GCSE English Language Specification A or the Edexcel Certificate in English Language. The exams you will face depend on which qualification you are taking.

All students will sit Paper 1:

- unprepared non-fiction

- Section A of the anthology

- writing to inform, explain and describe.

Certificate students and Route 1 Specification A students will sit Paper 2 for their specification:

- Section B of the anthology

- writing to explore, imagine and entertain *and* writing to argue, persuade and advise. Certificate students cover both triplets in two shorter answers but the Route 1 Specification A students have a choice and write on either triplet, not both.

Route 2 Specification A students will not sit Paper 2 but instead will complete coursework. Students of the Certificate in English Language will also have a coursework aspect to their course, but only the Speaking and Listening element.

Paper 1 and Paper 2 will not take place in the same sitting.

Make sure you are familiar with what to expect when you enter the exam hall – know which part of the exam you are sitting and you will feel more confident and prepared.

Check you know how long the paper lasts and think about how long that gives you on each section, including time to plan and read over your work. You will have 45 minutes for each section of Paper 1 and Paper 2.

Using exam language

Think carefully about how you answer the questions in your exam – your audience for these answers is an exam marker. This will be an experienced teacher, so try to make your language suit your audience:

- Keep your answers formal and steer away from language that may not be understood by everybody, such as words used in text messaging. Some writing tasks will specify an audience, form and purpose so there may be occasions where a less formal style is appropriate (e.g. a magazine article for young people). However, even then, too much informal language is not a good idea if you are going to show a range of vocabulary.

- Ensure that you are using the right technical language – e.g. don't confuse a metaphor with a simile! There is a glossary in the back of this book so revise these terms in advance and make sure you are comfortable using them.

- Think about varying your vocabulary, especially in the writing sections of the papers.

- Don't refer to authors by their first name – it is unlikely you know them so keep it formal and refer to them by their surname or as 'the writer' or 'the author'.

Tips and techniques

In the reading sections of the paper:

- Before you even look at the questions, make sure you know what the purpose, audience and techniques are for each extract – use your skimming, scanning and intensive reading skills for this.

- You are *not* marked on spelling or punctuation in the reading section.

- Make sure you have understood the question properly – check the key words and think about what the examiner is looking for.

- Check whether the question asks for a quotation or an example. If it does, make sure you put one in.

- Don't generalise! Phrases such as 'eye-catching' and 'makes it stand out' will not get you any marks – you have to be specific and give details about why something is eye-catching or stands out.

- In your revision you should consider different interpretations of the texts and their meanings so that you are prepared to fully explore a writer's possible intentions.

In the writing sections of the paper:

- Create a plan before you start writing.

- Be prepared for the different writing types – ensure you know the conventions of each style. You could jot a list at the top of your plan so you remember to use them. Here is an example of the list you might write for writing to describe:

   o alliteration

   o metaphor

   o single-word sentence

   o onomatopoeia.

- Think about your timings and stick to them.

- Leave a few minutes at the end to read over your work and, in that time, try to focus on improving at least ten of the words you have used – think about showing the examiner how powerful and varied your vocabulary is.

- If you've finished early, use the time to check your work again, make sure you've answered the question and improve it where you can.

- First and last sentences are important for making an impact on the reader, so think carefully about how you structure them and the lasting impression you want to create.

What the examiner wants

Examiners are not as scary as they may sometimes seem – they do really want you to do well! When you are in the exam, keep in mind the following points to ensure you get the best mark possible:

- Make sure your writing is legible. If the examiners cannot read it, they cannot mark it.

- Try to remember what the assessment objectives for the exam are. If you know which skill you are being tested on, you can make sure you are achieving it.

- Look at the marks for the questions. If it's a two-mark question, don't write a long essay. The examiner wants to see that you understand the requirements of the question.

- Make sure you plan. If you plan your answer, it will have a structure that will allow the examiner to follow your points, making it easier to award you marks.

- Answer the question. Make sure you understand the question and that you answer it! Sometimes people read it wrongly and write something that is not relevant to the question, losing marks needlessly.

- Check your answer over for silly mistakes.

- Remember that the examiner is expected to mark positively. They reward the good things you do rather than taking marks away for what you don't do.

Notes

Glossary

active and passive   Many verbs can be used actively or passively. 'The man smashed the window' is active. 'The window was smashed by the man' is passive. In the first sentence, the attention is on the man who performs the action. In the second sentence, the attention is taken away from the man and placed on the window. In many passive sentences, the person or thing responsible for the action is unknown or may not be identified at all, e.g. 'The money was stolen.' Passive forms are often used for formal and impersonal writing, e.g. 'It was stated that...' They may feature in writing such as reports of science experiments, or other writing where the person who performs the act is irrelevant.

alliteration   Where adjacent or closely connected words begin with or contain the same consonant sound, e.g. 'a long, lazy, lilting...', 'babbling brook'.

ambiguity   A phrase or statement that has more than one possible interpretation, such as this news headline: 'Climber Hurt on Face'. Ambiguity can often be the basis for jokes and may be accidental or deliberate.

anecdote   A story from personal experience. This is a useful way of supporting points you make in your own writing.

argument   A series of points put together to construct a clear case.

assonance   The repetition of vowel sounds in words that are close to each other, e.g. 'Hear the la**r**k and ha**r**ken to the ba**r**king.'

audience   The person or people for whom a text is intended. They may be defined by age, interest, existing knowledge, gender or any other linking characteristic.

autobiography   The story of someone's life (or part of that life), written by the actual person, sometimes with the help of a 'ghost writer'.

character   In literature, an imaginary person whose personality is formed by the author through description of their actions, what they say and what others say about them. Physical description and dress can give additional clues about character.

chronological writing   Writing organised in sequence, by order of time.

cliché   An over-used phrase, such as 'a close shave'. Sometimes these may also be idiomatic (see **idiom**).

colloquial   Relating to conversation and/or language used in familiar, informal contexts. Contrasted with formal or literary language.

discussion text   A text that outlines the different views on an issue. Sometimes such texts may adopt a 'for and against' structure before reaching a final conclusion.

ellipsis   The omission of words that are needed in order to complete the meaning of a phrase or sentence. This can be done deliberately to leave the reader in suspense. It is indicated by the use of three dots (...).

emotive language   Language used by a writer when trying to express their emotions in a personal way. Emotive language often produces an emotional response in the reader.

empathy   The ability to identify with a person or animal and so understand how he, she or it feels.

evaluation   A judgement about whether something is effective.

exclamation   A word or words that are suddenly uttered, perhaps in joy, pain, sadness or surprise. Indicated by the use of an exclamation mark (!).

explanatory text   An explanatory text tries to explain why something is as it is, and so will make use of causal connectives such as 'because', 'so' and 'therefore'.

fact   A fact is something that can be proven or demonstrated to be true and can be backed up with evidence. Sometimes opinions are presented as facts, particularly in persuasive writing.

figurative language   Language used to create vivid and dramatic effects where the meaning of words is not the same as their literal meaning. It will often make use of metaphor and simile, e.g. 'As a tailor, he was a cut above the rest.' Phrases like these may also be called figures of speech, e.g. 'Break a leg' which means 'good luck'.

form   The kind and style of writing required for a particular purpose or characteristic of a certain genre (e.g. article, letter, report).

formal/informal writing   Certain situations, e.g. a job application, require a particular style of writing. A letter to a friend would be more informally written. But remember, whomever the question asks you to address, you are writing for an examination, so do not be too informal – e.g. using slang would not be appropriate.

format   The style and arrangement of a text, indicating whether it is a book, a leaflet, a poster or another format. Within texts, format also relates to structure and may include use of columns, text boxes, diagrams, illustrations and so on.

genre and generic structure   Different text types conform to certain conventions of language, layout and purpose. Texts that share the same conventions are said to be in the same genre. Readers often recognise these patterns and use them to shape their expectations about what a certain text will contain and how it will be written. For example, a poem will have a different layout from a novel, and a newspaper article will have a different purpose from a graphic novel.

idiom   An expression that can be understood only as a whole, and where the intended meaning is not the same as the literal meaning of the words. An example is 'He let the cat out of the bag', which means that the person said something that should have been kept secret. Idioms add richness and variety to language and are a form of figurative language.

imagery   The use of language to create pictures in the minds of readers, often by using simile and metaphor.

imperative   The form of a verb used to give instructions or commands, e.g. 'Do your homework'.

information text   An information text seeks to give information, i.e. telling someone something they don't already know. An example is a report on an actual event.

instruction text   Instruction texts differ from explanation texts in that they tell the reader how to do a certain thing. As such, they will often use the imperative form of the verb, e.g. 'Take three eggs; break them into a bowl.' The steps must take place in a specific order, so vocabulary relating to chronology, sequencing and time will feature.

irony   Something that is contradictory in a surprising or humorous way because of the gap between the literal and implied meaning, e.g. 'Ironically, the anti-smoking campaigner ended up getting throat cancer – sheer bad luck: a cigarette had never once passed her lips.'

jargon   Words or expressions used by a particular group or profession, often specialist in nature, that are not usually understood by those outside the group, e.g. the military use the term AWOL which means 'Absent without leave'.

metaphor   A way of describing something by saying that it is another thing rather than merely like another thing, e.g. 'The sprinter was an express train, hurtling towards the finishing line.'

narrative text   A text that seeks to retell a story or event, and as such may often be prose fiction. Such texts will tend to use temporal connectives and stress sequence and chronology of events.

non-chronological writing   A form of writing, such as reports, in which sequence and chronology are not the predominant organisational features, e.g. a film script which contains flashbacks.

objective   When you write objectively you base your points on facts and not on your feelings. An analytical piece of writing, where you consider both sides of an argument, would have to be objective.

onomatopoeia   Words that imitate or suggest what they stand for, e.g. 'bang', 'cuckoo', 'pop'.

opinion   A belief or judgement that may be strongly held but which has yet to be proved.

paragraph   A self-contained section of text with a number of linked sentences contributing to a distinct set of ideas or information. The start of a paragraph is usually indicated, in a handwritten text, by beginning the first line slightly in from the left-hand margin, but can also be shown by a space between paragraphs.

person   In speech and writing we distinguish who we are referring to by using the first-person, second-person and third-person: the first person refers to oneself (I/we); the second person refers to one's listener or reader (you) and the third person refers to somebody or something else (he/she/it/they).

personification   A way of giving things or ideas human characteristics, e.g. 'Death stalked the battlefield.'

persuasive text   A form of writing that seeks to sway the opinions of the reader to agree with those of the writer, or persuade the reader to take some action. It will typically consist of a statement and supporting evidence, but may often present opinions as facts and may assume a shared agreement where none exists, e.g. 'Of course, we all know that UFOs really do exist.'

pun   A playful use of language that relies on homophony – different words sounding the same. It is frequently used in newspaper headlines and jokes, e.g. 'You can tune a guitar but you can't tuna fish.'

rhetorical question   Especially in speeches or other types of talk, a question that is for effect rather than to seek an answer. The speaker often wishes to persuade the audience that something is obvious or unanswerable, e.g. 'What have the Romans ever done for us?' Also, an expression used to make a point in a strong way.

scanning (text)   A form of rapid reading in which the reader quickly looks over a text in order to locate a specific piece of information.

sentence   Sentences are may be simple, compound or complex. A simple sentence consists of a single clause, e.g. 'I like eggs.' A compound sentence has two or more clauses joined by the words 'and', 'or', 'but' or 'so', e.g. 'I like eggs but I don't like bacon.' A complex sentence is one with a main clause and one or more other clauses that are of lesser importance than the main clause, e.g. 'Although the garden was well looked after, the weeds grew everywhere.'

setting   The time (day, date or year) and location of a story. It could also include the social and/or cultural conditions.

simile   An image created by describing something by comparing it to something else using the words 'like' or 'as', e.g. 'She sang as sweetly as a bird.'

skim   A way of reading quickly in order to get an overview of, or the gist of, a text.

slang   Words or phrases that are very informal and are used for vividness.

Standard English   Standard English is that which is considered the usual or accepted form of grammar and expression. It is not specific to any region and has no connection with accent.

subjective   When you write subjectively you are influenced by personal feelings and opinions. In subjective writing the author is giving his/her personal views on an issue.

summary   A short version of a longer piece of writing (such as a book or article), giving only the main points.

symbol   Something used to represent another thing or idea that also suggests or embodies other characteristics. For example, lions are often used as symbols of courage.

theme   A subject about which a person is speaking or writing. The theme may not be explicitly stated but will be a linking idea that connects the events and ideas in a piece of writing.

tone   The writer's attitude to a topic and the mood of a piece of writing.

topic sentence   A sentence, often at the start of a paragraph, that defines what the paragraph will be about and so orientates the reader as they begin the paragraph.

viewpoint   The point of view from which the story is told.

voice   The narrator of the text, either a first person narrator (who forms part of the events), or a third person narrator who is unidentified.

Index

Headings in **bold** are glossary terms.